I0793395

Midwest Maniacs

Tom Baker

Schiffer Publishing Ltd®

4880 Lower Valley Road, Atglen, Pennsylvania 19310

Dedication

This book is dedicated to the Thin Blue Line: the dedicated and courageous men and women of law enforcement.

Acknowledgments

I would like to thank my family, my editor Dinah Roseberry, John Titchenal, Adam Glass, Jason Leonard, Dayna Winters, and the hosts of *Spirit Finders Paranormal Radio* for their care and assistance at this time.

Text by author
Cover image courtesy www.bigstockphoto.com

Other Schiffer Books By The Author:
Indiana Ghost Folklore, ISBN / 978-0-7643-3343-7, $14.99
Scary Urban Legends, ISBN / 978-0-7643-3587-7, $14.99
Haunted Indianapolis, ISBN / 978-0-7643-2747-6, $14.99

Schiffer Books are available at special discounts for bulk purchases for sales promotions or premiums. Special editions, including personalized covers, corporate imprints, and excerpts can be created in large quantities for special needs. For more information contact the publisher:

Published by Schiffer Publishing Ltd.
4880 Lower Valley Road
Atglen, PA 19310
Phone: (610) 593-1777; Fax: (610) 593-2002
E-mail: Info@schifferbooks.com

For the largest selection of fine reference books on this and related subjects, please visit our website at **www.schifferbooks.com**
We are always looking for people to write books on new and related subjects. If you have an idea for a book, please contact us at proposals@schifferbooks.com

This book may be purchased from the publisher.
Include $5.00 for shipping.
Please try your bookstore first.
You may write for a free catalog.

In Europe, Schiffer books are distributed by
Bushwood Books
6 Marksbury Ave.
Kew Gardens
Surrey TW9 4JF England
Phone: 44 (0) 20 8392 8585; Fax: 44 (0) 20 8392 9876
E-mail: info@bushwoodbooks.co.uk
Website: www.bushwoodbooks.co.uk

Copyright © 2011 by Tom Baker

Library of Congress Control Number: 2011938795

All rights reserved. No part of this work may be reproduced or used in any form or by any means—graphic, electronic, or mechanical, including photocopying or information storage and retrieval systems—without written permission from the publisher.

The scanning, uploading and distribution of this book or any part thereof via the Internet or via any other means without the permission of the publisher is illegal and punishable by law. Please purchase only authorized editions and do not participate in or encourage the electronic piracy of copyrighted materials.

"Schiffer," "Schiffer Publishing Ltd. & Design," and the "Design of pen and inkwell" are registered trademarks of Schiffer Publishing Ltd.

Designed by Mark David Bowyer
Type set in HansHand / New Baskerville BT

ISBN: 978-0-7643-3942-4
Printed in the United States of America

Contents

Introduction

"Crimes of which a people is ashamed constitute its real history. The same is true of man."

~Jean Genet

Why do some men feel compelled to do evil? And what, exactly, constitutes evil? When men kill each other on a battlefield, under the banner of some nation, we proclaim them heroes if they survive, martyrs if they do not. If men kill for a cause, it would seem, it is considered genuine, just and noble.

If men kill for sport, it is considered the basest form of evil, and an affront to society. Likewise, if greed is the motive. But, of course, we can find many motives in many different types of violence and killing, and often there are no clear points of demarcation between what is just and noble, scandalous and predatory. There are, however, uncomfortable gray areas.

Abortion is hailed by some as being "pro-choice," by others as outright murder. Likewise, the death penalty is condemned by many as an inhuman and barbaric practice, best relegated to the bygone era when we boiled people in oil and burned witches at the stake. Yet it is still practiced, and lauded by some as a "deterrent" to crime (although there is no real evidence of this). Man has a bloodlust that yearns to be sated, and a moral imperative to justify this same lust by being either on the "right" or "wrong" side of society.

Society sets the boundaries for what is acceptable and unacceptable killing, what forms of bloodlust can be safely indulged (boxing and brutal sports for instance), and what forms of savagery lie so far beyond the pale of human reasoning that they demand swift and unyielding justice. So be it. Sanity is statistical.

Of course, there are many men and women who have transgressed the boundary between what is acceptable outlet for the "beast within," and what is simply giving into the baser impulses that, most hope, are bred out of each human animal through a long program of social conditioning. Such people can often be brilliant: the acclaimed writers Marquis De Sade and Jean Genet come to mind. Both men, while not being killers, were at the least criminals who spent many years in prison before finally finding that precious prism of self-actualization that transformed them from the petty ranks of common thugs; they became men whose words and visions would outlast their own bodily deaths. But such men are the exception.

Likewise, the writer William S. Burroughs, who shot his wife to death in an "accident," and maintained a heroin habit while living one step ahead of the law for much of his life. Burroughs would go on to write the classic novel of Beat generation rebellion *Naked Lunch*, and what would emerge from his experience as a man that often lived outside the law, and outside the conventions of society, was a literary vision that allowed him to give vent to the bestial inside, to explore those nether regions that society has marked off as taboo. Burroughs managed to turn the beast inside of himself into a domesticated and complacent animal, the better to serve his literary bents. But many hundreds of thousands do not have that option.

Herein lays the crux of the present volume.

We have assembled, for your education and delectation, a sample of some of the Midwest's most atrocious and vile human beings, a history of murder and mayhem committed by individuals that, unlike Jean Genet or William Burroughs, could not find it within themselves to sublimate the beast with a burning inner-vision of creativity or self-actualization. No indeed, the individuals whose stories are recounted here are the American Heartland's own sordid cabal, carefully hand-picked as a representation as to what depths a person can plumb before they are either captured like an animal, or meet death through their own sheer folly.

The individual stories recounted here are of people who were each born with the same capacity for self-realization as any other individual. Yet, inside themselves, the burning anger and contempt for societal norms, and the macabre visions of their own personal demons drove them, each, to committing acts so vile and reprehensible they earned for themselves a place in the annals of criminal history. These are their stories.

Draw what conclusions you may.

Micajah and Wiley Harpe

"Many years ago, two men named Harpe, appeared in Kentucky, spreading death and terror wherever they went. Little else was known of them but that they passed for brothers, and came from the borders of Virginia. They had three women with them, who were treated as wives, and several children, with whom they traversed the mountainous and thinly settled parts of Virginia into Kentucky marking their course with blood. Their history is wonderful, as well from the number and variety, as the incredible atrocity of their adventures..."

~ James Hall

Two men stand, lion-like, in the annals of early criminal lore: the Depraved Duo, Micajah and Wiley Harpe.

These terrible sons of thunder, born under a black moon in 1768 and 1770 respectively, have earned for themselves a place in the annals of human infamy; they degenerated from their time as robber bandits living with tribes of Indians, to full-fledged maniacal murderers with a taste for blood and vengeance.

Micajah (known as "Big" Harpe, while his cousin Wiley was known as "Little") was a strapping gorilla of a man from Knoxville, Tennessee, whose relatives had originally come over from Scotland. He and his brother were both Tories.

They lived on a farm with three women, apparently two wives and one common woman they both used for sexual purposes. The fun (if it can be called that) started in the fall of 1798, and would leave a bloody trail of forty bodies in its wake.

***

Let us imagine, for a moment, how the scene must have played out:

The man threw his hat into the dirt as he stood out in the barren, run-to-riot yard of the dilapidated farm.

"Harpe! You filthy jackanapes, come on out here and meet your justice!"

The man stamped angrily in the dirt as the women looked out the window in terror. The Harpe brothers had already begun packing their belongings. In time, the man outside was joined by others. Wiley figured he could hold them off with buckshot until they had time to make their escape into the surrounding countryside.

Already, the Harpe boys were known as fierce, vindictive, and scurrilous men. No one in the vicinity of Beaver Creek really wanted to tangle with them. Violence was all they had ever really known, the only schooling they had ever had, and they were fierce.

They had been a couple of eager rapists after the Revolution, having hooked up with several gangs of freebooters and Indians, and it was here that they first learned the casual art of inflicting pain and death with impunity. They were, to be blunt, no strangers to the savage.

Now, however, it seemed like they might become the victims of savagery themselves if they didn't hurry. They quickly hustled their three wives and what they could carry onto an old wagon, and tried to make good their escape.

It was not long, however, before they were set upon by the posse that had gathered outside their farmhouse door hours before. Even the wily Harpes had to admit that they were plum cooked.

The women were tied along with both of the brothers, and marched forward back to town. Apparently, the mob didn't intend to lynch them, but was intent on getting them back to the jail, so they could face proper justice.

It was while on this lonesome journey toward justice that the Harpe brothers made a daring attempt at escape. It succeeded. And that, as they say, is when the real fun began.

***

It was a dismal pit of a place, a "rowdy groggery," a tavern, but the Harpe brothers drew up on their horses. Inside, or so they suspected, they would find the man responsible for leading the posse onto their trail. Of course, they *had* stolen the horses as they were so accused, but that didn't really matter; they had been ratted out. And the man they suspected had done it was right beyond the tavern door.

Big Harpe stepped inside, his eyes peering around the room. Men shuddered to see him; word had already spread that he was a wanted man. The silence was thick and heavy in the place as he stormed across the floor toward a table in the back.

At the table, playing cards with a wooden stein in front of him, was Johnson. Whether Johnson was actually guilty of what Big Harpe suspected him of or not can only be known to God, but it hardly changes what happened later.

"Get up from that seat Johnson. I need to have a word with you. Outside."

Johnson thought of pulling his flintlock pistol, but thought better of it. Big Harpe would certainly be able to wrestle it away from him; the big bear was quick as a snake and just as ruthless. No, thought Johnson; it would be better to just play along for now, and see what the man wanted.

He got up from the table and walked outside. He suddenly felt the cold end of a gun at his back.

"We know what you did, you scoundrel. Now, march!"

Big Harpe walked his victim over to the surrounding brush, where Little Harpe was waiting. Little Harpe moved forward and slugged Johnson on the head with the end of a stick, knocking him out cold. Then, the duo tied up their quarry, threw him over the back of a horse, and rode away into the night.

***

It was later, while the water lapped at the edges of the lake in the moonlight, that they would decide just what to do with the body.

Johnson they had tied and gagged; he was just coming to.

He began to squirm and moan. They could hear him, through the buckskin gag, begin to beg for his life.

"Quiet, you gutless varmint! If you hadn't have let on about our horse thieving, you wouldn't be in this mess right now. Isn't that right, Micah?"

Big Harpe looked off at the pretty way the moon reflected off the surface of the lake. The natural music of crickets filled the air. Out here, a man could get back to himself, to some semblance of normal communion with nature and the animal forces that were the heart and soul of men such as himself. He spat tobacco juice, said, "Ayup! It sure is, Wile. And I'll tell you something else. A man that would betray his comrades in such a dastardly, cowardly fashion as this here Johnson–"

And he motioned at the bound and gagged man laying on the ground at the edge of the water. (The man squirmed, working in cold terror against his bonds. Working in vain.)

"Well, that sort of man deserves a sort of punishment that is special. The sort of punishment that God, in His infinite wisdom, might have delivered on the head of a Philistine in the pages of the Good Book. He deserves pain, and torment and an agonizing death like few men have ever experienced. Ain't that right, Wile?"

Wile laughed, suddenly, feeling his pulse quicken as he prepared to do what they had come there to do. The victim, rolling around in terror in the tall weeds and grasses, now began to try and inch away comically, like a worm, from the impending death he knew he could not escape.

The knife gleamed in the moonlight.

Wiley looked at it, a silver, mad gleam entering his eye. Johnson could not believe how animalistic, how cruel that face suddenly seemed to become. It was like Wiley and his brother had taken on the features of the Devil himself.

"Do you want to do the honors, Micah? Or should I?"

"Maybe we should toss for it?"

They did.

Big Harpe won the honors.

They dragged Johnson toward them by the feet.

They ripped open the front of his shirt.

They slowly sliced him neck to pelvis.

Then they cut through clean to his spine.

Then they disemboweled him.

***

Afterward, wiping the blood off their hands, the two men considered what they had done. Big Harpe said to Little Harpe, "What you want to do with the body, Wile?"

Wily Harpe considered a moment, then said, "Well, I reckon we got to put him in the river, but we should weight him down first. Here, fetch up some of them rocks, some of the bigger ones, and lets fill his chest in with some of them. That will weight the body down and make it to stay underwater."

Big Harpe got an exultant look on his bearded, wild face.

"My, that sure is a plum good idea, Wile! And, what's more, if this here fellow is ever found, it will be know'd by all and sundry that we did it, as it is our own unique style. Man alive, I guess I understand now why Mama always said you got all the brains."

"Well, that's why they named me 'Wiley'. Wiley means 'brains', and I got plenty of 'em."

The idiotic pair made good their plans, filling up the gaping chest cavity of the cadaver with stones before floating the body out to the middle of the lake. It was a few days later that it was discovered.

The pair then headed toward Cumberland Gap to claim their women.

***

No one is certain, specifically, what started them on the murder spree that would claim upwards of forty victims, but it seems that after the sadistic job they had done on Johnson, the Harpes just developed a taste for dealing out death. On the way to their romantic reunion, they killed a pair of travelers from Maryland, with a possible motive of robbery. This was on the Wilderness Road, and it was here that they would also claim a victim named Langford. It was December 13th, 1799.

***

Mr. Langford got off his horse, heaved a dusty sigh, went through the door of the Inn, and pounded on the bar.

"Innkeeper! Food and drink please, I'm starving!"

Mr. Langford sat his bulk down on a stool. The innkeeper huffed and puffed his way through the darkness at the back of the bar, preparing some food and drink for his impatient guest.

"Hold on to your breeches! I can't be expected to work that fast!" said the fat innkeeper.

In the darkness, playing cards at a table, were the Brothers Harpe. They caught sight of Langford jiggling a leather pouch of silver at his side. Wiley Harpe leaned over to his brother and whispered.

"Sure must be carrying some amount, do you think?"

"Aye. Might do us a little good to check up on him after he leaves."

That they did. They killed Mr. Langford in exactly the same way that they had killed the others, cutting open the chest cavity and filling it with stones. This time, though, they did not bother to try and sink the body in water, but simply left it hidden, where it was found only a short time later.

***

After the killing of Langford, the Harpes were captured on Christmas day of 1799 and imprisoned in Langford, Kentucky. They managed to break out of jail almost immediately, leaving their three pregnant wives behind (the women were each found not guilty and released, fleeing a lynch mob to later rejoin their husbands), and took up with a band of outlaws that was busily being pursued in western Kentucky. They robbed and killed all along the way.

One of their victims was the son of Colonel Daniel Trabue. Another group were three or four hapless campers shot near the fire "near the mouth of the Saline River." The Harpes killed indiscriminately and at a whim, and victims are estimated to be as many as forty.

It was while fleeing a posse that the Harpes fell in with pirates along Cave-in-Rock, a strange series of caverns occupied by local buccaneers who made their living robbing flatboats on the Ohio River. The Harpes, by this time described as being "more animal than human," were welcomed by the scurvy pirates with open arms... Until one night when the Harpes got the creative idea of how to dispose of a sole prisoner.

"We're gonna take the miserable sumbitch up to the top of the cliff, tie him to a horse, and let rip!"

Their fellow pirates at first thought that they were joking. The Harpes did just as they promised. The pirates decided that this was too much, even for them.

The Harpes and their women had to go.

***

When the end finally came for the Harpe brothers, it was as gruesome as might be expected.

After laying low for awhile, they cut a swath of death across Tennessee, murdering a farmer named Bradbury, a little girl, a passing slave, an entire migrating family, a youth who was struck through the head with a hatchet, and another man who was killed in the customary way of being hollowed out and filled with stones.

Indeed, the entire final body count attributable to the Harpes may never be known.

Stopping with a posse in close pursuit, Little Harpe was annoyed by the sound of one of his children fussing for food. He promptly swung the child by the legs into the trunk of a tree, braining her.

After committing a mass slaughter at the Stegall home, which included Mrs. Stegall, her baby, Major William Love, an overnight guest, and another man named Trowbridge, Big and Little Harpe soon found themselves surrounded by the local militia (one of many posses that were hunting them), and found themselves unable to extricate themselves from their predicament.

The militia laid hands on Big Harpe, cutting off his head immediately, an act that is described to have "left him laughing."

"Hurry it up! Oh, you're a fine one! I'll see you all in hell!"

These are the sorts of things Big Harpe is reported to have screamed as he was decapitated. His head was later nailed to a tree as a grim warning to passersby. Hence, the area of Tennessee where this grim execution was enacted has become known as Harpe's Head Hill. We suppose it is probably haunted.

Little Harpe, amazingly, managed to escape, and rejoined his pirate friend Captain Mason before finally, according to legend, stabbing the man in the back (literally) and taking his head for the reward money.

This was a mistake on the part of Little Harpe, as the posse immediately recognized him as being one of the Harpe brothers, hanged him, and then cut off his head. And what do you think they did with *his* head?

Like his ill-fated brother, they nailed his noggin to a tree.

Reportedly, the Harpe wives lived out the remainder of their lives under assumed names, peacefully.

The Bloody Benders

The scene was like something out of a supernatural novel.

The assembled group sat around an old table in a tiny cottage. On the table there was an assortment of items: a trumpet, a tambourine, and some personal items belonging to someone's deceased relative. The sitters were all clasping hands, while the medium, a young, attractive lady named Kate Bender, closed her eyes and concentrated on contacting her Red Indian guide.

Finally, she began to speak in a voice that was shockingly unlike her own.

One of the sitters gasped. A cold hand had emerged from the darkness and laid itself on her shoulder. Suddenly, several of the sitters became rather fearful as they saw the metal trumpet rise of its own accord and seemingly float around the table, issuing forth with a strange, metallic whisper.

"Hello mother! It has been so long since last we spoke, and it is so beautiful here on this side!"

The voice echoed out in the room, and the woman to whom the voice was speaking began to cry, wanting desperately to believe that this was the voice of her late daughter. A translucent form seemed to appear in the darkness, a ghostly figure of ectoplasm that emitted from the astral body of the medium.

Or so the sitters thought.

***

The "spirit" in this case was none other than the medium's dim-witted brother, dressed up in flowing chiffon, and walking slowly around the room, touching people with nervous clammy fingers in the darkness.

Kate fancied herself an actual medium, felt she could communicate with the dead, and even heal people of their illnesses, but she wasn't beyond resorting to the crude methods of trickery when it suited her financial needs. Her family was very oriented toward making money. In fact, that was why they had opened this little inn in their own home to begin with.

Kate took her mediumistic act to several Kansas towns, and her physical attributes were as interesting to some of the male sitters as her alleged paranormal powers. These physical charms brought the men a-calling to the Bender residence, brought them to the plentiful table kept by Ma Bender. Tonight, it was a séance (which the sitters had generously paid for with donations) that was being held, but any other night of the week it might be a handsome beau with hopes of courtship, or a dusty traveler of the plains who stopped by for a hot meal and a bed.

The price, though, in many cases, was much higher than the customers had ever intended to pay.

***

The young man seated himself at the table. Before him, a delicious meal was spread out on the rickety wood. He may have come seeking the attentions of Kate Bender, or he may have been traveling the prairie as a drifter, hoping to put down a homestead on the wide, yawning plains of Kansas. Whatever the case, he had money on him, and the Benders knew it.

Old Man Bender seated himself at the head of the table, while Ma Bender and Kate set the dishes down on the table and heaped out the food on the young man's plate.

"Well, my-my, that's enough to make a man weep. Why, I don't remember when was the last time I had a decent meal."

"Well," said Kate, seating herself with a little sigh. "I sure hope you eat your fill tonight. We've made enough for twenty people I think."

The man smiled, leaning back in his chair.

"And might I say you are looking lovely tonight, Kate?"

Father Bender looked over at his wife with a knowing look, almost a scowl. Ma Bender said, "You quit that Will! You're going to give somebody a swelled head!" Ma Bender blushed a little, but Kate seemed to really enjoy the praise. The young man said, "Well, a girl that pretty ought to have herself a swelled head. I don't see any harm in it."

Grace was quickly said, and the young man began to ladle food into his mouth. He realized, for the first time, that he was sitting with his back to the long canvas sheet that divided the cabin in half. He stopped chewing momentarily and cocked his head. He thought he could hear footsteps back there, maybe even breathing.

"Say, what is going on back there behind the curtain, Ma? Seems as if someone is back there behind me."

He felt a strange sense of fear creep over him.

"Say, I think I'm going to move to another seat. Ma, would it be okay if I traded places with you at the table?"

The Benders looked at each other with alarm. Kate Bender, usually so pretty and prim and proper, suddenly blurted out, "No, you don't! You are going to sit right there and finish dinner, do you understand me?"

The man looked completely bewildered now. Kate was staring at him with flaming eyes and flaring nostrils. He mumbled something, and continued to eat, a little unsure of himself now, and morose from being scolded. The sheet rustled again, the breathing became heavy. Suddenly, he heard a swishing behind the curtain.

Stars exploded behind his eyes.

The world went black.

A body slumped, bleeding, over the table.

Dim-witted John Bender threw the canvas aside and dragged the body back across the curtain. Old Man Bender started yelling at him, snapping his fingers, "Get him off the table before he bleeds all over everything!"

Ma and Kate sat in silence for a moment. Then, they began to eat again, slowly.

***

The body was dragged back to a trap door and dumped down into the root cellar.

The floor of the cellar was always reeking of dried blood. This was not the first time a body had been unceremoniously dumped down here. Later, they would have their idiot son, the family killer, drag the body out into the moonlight, and he and Old Man Bender would bury it in the cow pasture, beneath the Kansas moon.

***

Colonel York was concerned about his brother. The young man had not been seen at the family home for awhile, and as he understood it, the man was going to travel to see one of his patients who was dying of cancer, and that this patient was not far from the home. It would have been about a day's journey, Colonel York figured, and along the way his brother said he would be staying at the little inn operated by the Bender family. He had stayed there before, he claimed, and it was mighty homey.

Colonel York set out to the Benders to see if his brother had ever showed up. As he rode up to the place, Old Man Bender was standing out on the porch waiting for him, his thumbs behind his suspenders, smoking his pipe and looking a wee bit apprehensive.

"Can I help you?"

Colonel York got off his horse with a huff, and said, "Yes sir. You are Mr. Bender, I take it?"

"That I am. And who might you be, sir?"

The man took off his hat, and strode up to the porch. Right away, Old Man Bender could see that this fellow had an erect, military bearing about him.

"I'm Colonel York. My brother, Dr. William York, was riding through these parts. Said he was going to stay at your place overnight. Well, that was nigh on a week ago, and he ain't been heard from since."

Old Man Bender rubbed his scruffy chin, said, "Well, we ain't seed him around these parts. Ain't no one stayed with us for awhile now. Business has been kind of slow."

Colonel York looked at the old man suspiciously. He smelled something fishy in his demeanor, and he felt ill at ease all of a sudden.

"Say, you better go on and get a look on for your brother. He may have been got by the Indians. And, you know, Jesse James is about."

"Sure."

The old man seemed to not know what to say for a moment, and then said, "Say, if you want, you and me can drag the river. You think he might have gone in for a dip and got drowned?"

Colonel York looked off into the distance. He knew, instinctively, that something wasn't right.

"Possible, but I think unlikely."

The Colonel then said, "Say, Mr. Bender, you mind if I have a look around?"

Old Man Bender's eyes narrowed to slits and his mouth tightened up as he said, "No sir. Not at all. We don't like folks messing around on our property. What, are you trying to accuse us of something unseemly?"

"No, not at all it's just--"

"No two ways about it, sir! You've insulted myself and my family. Now get on out of here before I have to get my shotgun!"

Colonel York looked at the old man with a cobra's gaze for a moment, before mounting his horse. Before he rode off he vowed, "Sir, I may return with my friend, the Sheriff."

He did just that.

***

There was a posse that descended on the Bender place that May 3rd, 1873, but they found no Benders present: The family had packed up and moved with incredible speed. They even managed to take their cattle with them.

The posse entered the house, and it was not long before they discovered the secret room behind the canvas curtain, and the trap door that led downward, into a reeking hole of a cellar. A cellar, Colonel York noted grimly, that was stained with human blood.

The smell was heavy and sickening.

They began to inspect the cow pasture around the property. It was not long before they encountered eleven freshly dug mounds.

"Boys, I'll be sumbitch," said the Colonel. "Those look just like graves to you?"

His brother was in the first grave they dug up.

***

The Benders could have been anywhere; indeed, they stole enough money to hide out in comfort indefinitely. The law in Kansas pursued them for decades with no success. Finally, two women, alleged to be Ma and Kate Bender were brought in, in 1898, but their identities could never be sufficiently proven, and there was no trial.

There was, however, a legend.

It was rumored that a posse, indeed, caught up with the Benders.

What follows is, generally, what is alleged to have happened.

***

The family had been captured on the road while trying to make good their escape. The posse had shot Ma and Old Man Bender when first identified. John Bender, the idiot son, and Kate, were both bundled into a wagon with the bodies of their parents, and driven to some surrounding woods.

The leader of the posse might have been Colonel York (and if the story is to be any good, don't we have to imagine that it was?), but it could have been any burly, seasoned veteran of the Civil War, perhaps a man with a cowboy hat, a great beard, a buckskin coat, and a pair of leather gloves.

And a side-arm, of course.

The posse took their captives to the edge of an old field, near a mushy, shit-stinking cow pasture. They led John, hooded, with a rope around his idiot neck, to the edge of an old, rundown fence. The leader of the posse quickly pronounced sentence over the vicious killer of eleven men, and informed him, as John had probably already surmised, that his sentence was to be summary execution.

He quickly pointed his revolver at the bound and hooded young man, shooting him in the chest above the heart, and watching with some satisfaction as he fell against the fence post, writhed in pain for a moment, and then lay still.

They had reserved the most special and gruesome punishment for Kate, though, as it was thought, since she was a spiritualist, that she must surely be possessed by devils.

She began to roar at them,

"The spirits will punish you for this! My Lord, my death has finally come! The stars are in correct alignment!"

"Shut up, you Yankee whore!" some loyal ex-Confederate in the party may have shouted out; maybe the man surmised that no one but a "damn Yankee" could be responsible for such an atrocious series of crimes.

Whatever the case, Kate was quickly tied to an old fence post. Then, in what must have seemed like a scene from the Middle Ages, the company gathered together some firewood and burned her alive.

Of course, there is probably a ghost story connected with this particular legend. But we couldn't swear to it.

Does Kate Bender's restless spirit haunt some lonely stretch of Kansas prairie when the moon is full and the stars are "in alignment"?

We may never know for sure.

Belle Gunness

Belle Gunness was a lady fair,
From Indiana state,
She weighed about three hundred pounds,
And that is quite some weight

~Traditional folk ballad

Belle Gunness was never going to be happy with life "down on the farm."

She was never going to be satisfied with her husband, Peter Gunness, either. The stout woman found her lucky stars shining brightly one fine day, as a meat grinder mysteriously found itself embedded in his head, killing him instantly. The local coroner cried "foul play!," but a jury decided otherwise, and Belle was allowed to return home without any formal charges being filed.

Belle found herself a steady paramour soon after, in the form of skulking handyman Joe Lamphere.

Joe was a mighty formidable lover. Or at least, he was much more formidable than the luckless Peter Gunness. But Belle still faced a rather pressing concern: How was she going to keep her small hog farm from going under financially?

It was not long before the practical, pragmatic, and undeniably psychotic Belle would hit upon an idea, one that would lead her to the annals of criminal infamy.

***

Permit us to recreate what might have been the typical scenario as regards to the Belle Gunness murders.

A luckless man opens up the classified section of his newspaper, looking for something, anything that promises to break the dull monotony of his existence. His eyes carefully scan the small rows of type until he finally hits upon something that seems interesting. It is an ad in the "Lonely Hearts" column, apparently placed by a woman in Indiana who specified that "triflers need not apply." Whoee! Here was a woman looking to hitch up! The man gets up, still holding the paper in his hands, and goes to the mirror, taking a look at himself and wondering how best he can spruce himself up to present himself to the widow Gunness.

***

It is a long, dusty ride through the heartland, but finally, our man finds himself at the right place. Or so he thinks. He had stopped in LaPorte to water his horses and get directions out to the Gunness place, and locals have treated him a little oddly. Maybe folks around here just weren't as friendly as they were in other parts of the country.

The man rides right up to the front porch, past the scowling hulk chopping wood in the front yard. Suddenly, a stout, plain-faced woman appears on the porch, wiping her hands on an apron. As he gets closer he gets a look at her face and general portly-ness, and he doesn't like what he sees.

Oh well. He has come a long way, and danged if he isn't going to stop and catch a meal at lest before shoving off.

"Hello, darling, I'm Belle. I'm so pleased to meet you. It's so good of you to come. Come on in, I was just about to put supper on the table."

The man goes inside, a little hesitantly, noting the way he is shadowed by the hulking Joe Lamphere.

The man comes in and sits down, introducing himself to the children. All in all, he reckons them to be a pretty somber bunch; the children seem as sullen as Lamphere, and only Belle herself seems to be pleased that he is here. She does, however, seem a little cagey.

"Why don't you sit down and I'll fix you up a plate. We can say grace then. Joe here – he's my handyman – good ol' Joe, he'll lead us in prayer."

Belle does just as she promises, and Lamphere seats himself next to her, bowing his head and folding his huge, scarred hands as he closes his eyes and leads them in a word of prayer. The man feels his stomach begin to grumble. The food in front of him smells utterly delicious.

He begins to eat, famished, and indeed the food is very good. He has to give Belle at least one thing: what she lacks in looks, she makes up for in culinary talent. Funny, though, the food seems to have a strange under taste at times, a little ingredient he can't quite put his finger on. But it doesn't bother him, as it is not very noticeable.

Later, they are seated in the parlor, where Belle amuses the two men with stories and songs and little jokes. She plays the piano, and the man reclines on a couch, feeling sleepy and full. Joe Lamphere sits in a chair in the corner, scowling. Belle continues to play old time songs, wooing her potential paramour with the fierce intensity of her personal charms.

"And I just know you'll love this one. Why, we use to sing this one all the time when we were girls. My dear, are you feeling a little faint? Why don't you just lie down and relax. I'll have Joe turn the lights down for you, alright? There's a good fellow."

The luckless fellow lays back, feeling dizzy. The walls seem to be swimming, the lights growing dim as he fades out. He may have pleasant dreams in his drugged state, but, whether he has dreams or nightmares, they are nocturnal visions from which he will never again awake.

***

Joe would finish him off, usually by strangulation.

Then it would be time to dismember the body, and bury the parts.

Of course, their pigs got hungry, and needed to be slopped. What was an arm, a leg, a string of intestines to a hungry pig?

They were not apt to turn their snouts up to whatever they could get.

***

It was the coming of the Norwegian that spelled trouble and the end for Belle Gunness.

Or was it?

The man had come from South Dakota to meet Belle, having seen one of her ads in a Norwegian language newspaper. He quickly decided that this was a good prospect for finding a wife.

Like so many others, he learned how incorrect he was in this assumption.

This man had a brother, a Mr. Helgelian, whom he had told about his trip to Indiana to meet a woman. Mr. Helgelian, not having heard from his brother after that, realized something must be wrong. Fearfully, he read the ad that had sent his brother out on his fool's errand. He knew what he had to do.

He traveled out to the Gunness farm, but the old lady was tight-lipped, and the hulking handyman stood around her like a fearsome shadow. Mr. Helgelian was told that his brother had been sent away, that Joe Lamphere was going to be Belle's new husband, and that the Norwegian had not told her where he was headed.

"He did look mighty poorly when he left," she added, a might perturbed that someone would dare to come snooping around her farm asking questions.

Mr. Helgelian left, not feeling very good about the situation altogether. Nagging suspicions sent him to Sheriff Smutzer, who had had his suspicions about Belle ever since her husband had met with his untimely demise.

Then a curious thing happened.

***

The Sheriff walked around the smoking ruins, wondering what in the world to make of it all. The Gunness farmhouse was in a shambles, and the bodies of the three children were charred almost beyond recognition. They were still searching for the body of Belle.

What had started it? Well, he knew it could be damn near anything, but, the timing seemed awful suspicious to him. Why, all of a sudden, should this tragedy occur now, when Mr. Helgelian had rode into town looking for his lost brother at the Gunness place? No, Sheriff Smutzer didn't believe in bad coincidences, and this one was about the worst coincidence that he could possibly conceive of. He knew of only one man who could possibly answer any of his questions: Joe Lamphere.

They found him drinking at a local tavern, and collared him quickly. According to him, Belle had sent him away, and he knew little else. As he sweated it out under intense interrogation, it became more and more obvious to Sheriff Smutzer that Joe Lamphere knew a lot more than he was willing to admit to. It also became obvious that the onerous oaf was not going to let forth with a single peep about any of it.

Sheriff Smutzer was well-aware of the seedy reputation of Joe Lamphere. He was also dimly aware that Belle had tried to divest herself, only recently, of the handyman, and had let drop a hint that if anything should happen to her, they might go looking for Lamphere as a possible suspect.

"I'm warning you, if you don't come clean with me Joe, I'm going to charge you with the murder of Belle Gunness and her children. Do you understand what I'm telling you?"

At this the burly farm hand broke into a frenzy, protesting his innocence. "What! This is an outrage. I never had nothing to do with killing anybody, I swear!"

***

It was not long before those who were sifting through the ruins of Belle's house began to find odd trinkets, like six gold men's watches.

Also, human teeth.

Slivers of bone.

It seemed that Belle, whatever might have happened to her, had been up to no good.

When they got to digging in the hog pen, they found a few more grisly trophies.

Four bodies wrapped in oilcloth, butchered expertly.

And there was every indication that there might be more.

***

A prospector from California built a sluice on the property, and when the water went running through the ruins it unearthed even more strange treasures. Apparently, Belle had spent a considerable amount of time researching arcane subjects, such as hypnotism and rare poisons. The charred pages of books on these subjects washed up from the muddy ground, along with a number of toiletries and trinkets one would associate with many men.

Also, they unearthed ten more stinking stiffs.

Butchered men, martyrs to Belle's obsession with securing the financial resources necessary to finally ditch her decrepit pig farm and flee to more congenial climes. It appeared though, that Belle might be the final victim of her own madness. Or so Sheriff Smutzer surmised for a short time.

***

There was a problem.

The body that lay in the morgue, the body that had initially been assumed to be that of Belle Gunness, was just a little on the lean side. Belle was a heavy woman, near three hundred pounds, and this body was missing, according to the local coroner, about a hundred and fifty pounds of that. Of course, Belle might have discovered a new crash diet, but Sheriff Smutzer tended to doubt it.

"Well, would fire make a body shrink in that manner?" he had asked the coroner.

The man had shaken his head, and said, "No. Whoever this is, if you say your Belle Gunness was three hundred pounds, well, then this isn't her."

"Well, what about the gold tooth and the partial plate we found? I suppose she just decided to leave them behind?"

In fact, Sheriff Smutzer got the sneaking suspicion that this was exactly what Belle had done. He had the partial plate and gold tooth examined by the dentist who had made them, and it was confirmed that, indeed, they had belonged to Belle Gunness. Of course, it would be a small matter for Belle to go and leave her dentures behind.

So whose body was it exactly that they had in their morgue?

***

It would be many years, and a jail-house confession to a cell mate, before the truth about the final victims of Belle Gunness would finally come pouring out of Joe Lamphere.

"I done helped her with it all. We'd bring them out to the house with the ads, set 'em down to dinner, get 'em good and fed, and slip 'em cyanide in the food. Then, I'd finish them off. Belle liked to crush the heads, and the rest of it could go to the pigs, what we didn't bury. But, dang the old girl, she must have clean got away with it, as the body they found wasn't her. See, Belle was the sort of woman took up with other women sometimes, if you know what I mean. Well, she had this lover in Chicago, a little on the lean side, and she done have her come out to the farm, and she killed her just as sure as we killed all them men. Well, Belle poisoned her kids, too. Set the whole place on fire and, who knows? Maybe right now she is sunning herself up, enjoying all the cash we stole, while I'm sitting here in this damn cell."

***

Belle stole an estimated thirty thousand dollars from various men she'd killed. Some were conned into handing her over life's savings before she did them in. Others were simply robbed outright for whatever they had on them. All told, she got away (if she got away) with a phenomenal sum of money for those days.

***

Some had Belle as a whorehouse madam in Chicago.

Some sighted her as far away as Brazil.

Whatever the case, there can be little doubt that Belle, true to her homicidal nature, remained a criminal and killer to the very last. After all, if you don't even draw the line at killing your own children, what hope for you can there possibly be?

We must assume, God willing, she finally met justice, in the end.

H. H. Holmes

"In conclusion, I wish to say that I am but a very ordinary man ... and to have planned and executed the stupendous amount of wrongdoing that has been attributed to me would have been wholly beyond my power."

~Dr. H. H. Holmes

The career of Herman Webster Mudgett, better known during his lifetime by the alias H. H. Holmes, is one that defies credulity and, were it not truth, would be labeled the basest example of literary invention. The very details of the case itself: bigamy, fraud, theft, medical malpractice, and the construction of a huge, poorly-built, "murder castle" during the World's Fair of 1893, render the full range of Holmes' diabolical capability something to, truly, shudder at.

The early years of his life, spent as an outcast, overly intelligent, sulky boy under the tutelage of his stern, outwardly loveless parents, could hardly have provided a better background to the sordid development of a young man who would, in time, be regarded as America's first "serial killer."

There was admittedly something always "wrong" about young Mudgett: He was known to be a strange, brooding, maladaptive little tyro, whose chief interest, beside torturing small pets to death and dissecting them, seemed to be dominating his mentally slower peers and abusing them as a game of sport; or at the very least, taking unfair advantage of them.

This early activity as a scoundrel laid the groundwork for the rest of his life; he would, within the space of a few years, graduate to acts of forgery, fraud, and insurance scam.

He would finally earn his highest degree of proficiency in the art of murder.

Some of his earliest humbuggery revolved around the acquisition of phony patents for the sale of machines, the function of which, typically, could not be credited with the claims made against them. Also, it is reported that snake-oil and phony nostrums were not, altogether, out of his league, and must of appealed to the pretensions of a young man that would, in time, graduate from medical college a legitimate doctor.

(He was not, for long, to remain one.)

Medical school, undertaken right before his several bigamous marriages got underway, must have opened up a new facet of his distorted psyche, allowing him to confirm, outwardly, the inner contempt he felt for the rest of his fellow creatures . Here, in the darkened sanctity of the dissection chamber, he could autopsy cadavers at his leisure, coldly cutting free the skin, and fat, and inner organs of the deceased, and fondling them in wonder, amazed at the utilitarian nature of each and every fibrous molecule of the body. It was here, (indeed, it must have been here) while he was surrounded at the university morgue by the decayed remnants of life, that he first began to view the world through the pathological prism of the psychopathic killer, as well as that of the habitual con man.

One wonders, as he immersed himself in the delicate, and fragile workings of the body, if he ever evidenced any more than a passing recognition of the humanity that the decaying specimens had once represented. If so, it must have been for the last time, because, in future, he would grow to embrace the world of murder for profit with a zeal amounting to vengeance.

Holmes greatest contribution to the world of crime, and his sole contribution to the history of mass murder, was a three-story ramshackle building he erected in Chicago, in 1893, to serve as a hotel, primarily for naive young woman who came to town for the World's Columbia Exposition. It was a truly historic event in the life of old Chicago, and brought upwards of thirty million people into the Windy City, swamping local authorities in a deluge of petty crime and graft, and ensuring that H. H. Holmes would have a smorgasbord of grim picking from which to hone his deadly twilight trade into a veritable art form.

Holmes had first hit upon the idea, when, after coming to Chicago, he secured employment as a pharmacist, managing to steal away a small business from Mrs. E. S. Holten, who became enamored of Holmes' good looks and glib tongue. Of course, it was not long before Mrs. Holten and her more cautious daughter suddenly "disappeared to settle financial matters in another part of the country," and predictably were never seen again. We can well-imagine what their fate must have been, for Holmes quickly took over sole proprietorship of the pharmacy at 63rd and South Wallace, and immediately set his eyes on larger scams than pushing bottles of "Miracle Elixir" (these were largely little more than watered-down booze).

There was a space across the road that caught the apple of his eye, a place more than suitable to carry out the sort of "death factory" endeavor that was slowly taking shape in his mind. In short order, he began to line up a capital series of crimes and swindles to acquire the money to break the dirt, lay the foundation, and begin the arduous task of building what would become, to modern crime historians, the "Holmes Murder Castle."

To complete this task, Holmes found it necessary to employ the services of three separate building crews, all of whom, eventually, found themselves swindled by the financial machinations of the devious man.

That three separate construction crews were employed served to mask the real purpose behind many of the odd architectural features of the three-story, city-block long building. Why, for instance, gas pipes were required to reach into each separate guest room; why the walls of certain rooms were lined with asbestos; why one room was, essentially, simply a huge vault-like prison.

Accompanying the oddities, was the presence of a remarkable setup in the basement, which included a mammoth crematory, pits of quicklime in the concrete floor, a massive dissecting table, and a veritable cornucopia of macabre surgical instruments and poisonous chemicals, all ready to effect, for Dr. "Harry Howard Holmes" the supreme, casual, taking of a large swath of human life, for pleasure and profit.

His first victims were culled from the ranks of pretty young women who found themselves hopeful for secretarial work. Unluckily for them, they hit upon the demented Holmes as a possible employer.

His typical modus operandi involved immediate sexual advances on the prospective employee, which resulted, much of the time, in the unfortunate young women becoming enthralled with the tall, dashing rake hell. Seducing his prey, offering them the hopes of a prospective marriage after professions of instantaneous "love at first sight," Holmes managed to quicken the pulse of a seemingly endless succession of very naive young women.

After spending the night using his victims sexually, he would creep from bed, and casually walk to his office to retrieve chlorophyll. After sufficiently rendering the young woman unconscious, Holmes would then throw the body into a disused elevator shaft. Then after placing a single pane of glass over the doorway, and forthwith attaching a gas-pumping hose into a single hole, he could at his leisure, watch the awakening mistress suddenly struggle in panic, and then finally succumb to the asphyxiating effects of the gas.

In a few moments, after ventilation had thus assured the gas would be no threat to Holmes himself, he could lasso the girls neck, drag her upward, then dispose of her by means of a greased chute to his basement morgue, thereby proceeding to dismember, cremate, dispose of the remains in quicklime, and steal away to his private "laboratory" on the third floor to fondle and "experiment" on whatever parts of the corpse interested him most.

And the payoff in this macabre routine? Besides the sick gratification in wanton murder, it became known, later, that Holmes had coerced a number of the young women to sign over their savings and insurance to him.

The sun began to set on Holmes just a short while later, with the arrival of a young lady from Texas named Minnie Williams.

Minnie was from a wealthy family, but had decided to try Chicago out in the hopes of becoming a shining light of the American stage. When applying for room and board, she chanced, unfortunately, upon the Murder Castle and it's monstrous proprietor. It was only a short time later that Holmes convinced her that they should be married.

He also, predictably, encouraged her to sign over all her worldly possessions and holdings to him. For once, a woman had the temerity to say no to Holmes.

He did convince her, however, to contact her sister Nannie in Fort Worth, and to have her come and visit her and her successful, prospective husband in Chicago. At first, the strange threesome had a high time on

Holmes' ill-gotten gains, going on shopping sprees and dining in the finest restaurants in Chicago. But all was not to remain wine and roses, for it was only a short time later that Minnie and Nannie ran into, shockingly, an old mutual acquaintance who, when told that Minnie was engaged to a "Doctor Harry H. Holmes," was astounded to note that she had a friend herself in Wilmette who was married to a Dr. Harry Holmes.

Minnie confronted Holmes, remembering that, indeed, he had bragged at owning property in Wilmette, and it was not long before she put two and two together. The only witness to the ensuing debacle was the building janitor, who despite being locked out of Holmes' private world of torture and murder, saw and heard enough to arouse in himself mighty suspicions concerning the strange nature of his employer's activities.

Holmes, indeed, was married to a woman in Wilmette, as he was married to a woman in Indiana, and another woman in Philadelphia who he had murdered.

Of course, Nannie and Minnie Williams disappeared shortly after, and so did Holmes, but not before he had set fire to his own sprawling hotel in an attempt to collect on the insurance money. This did not go as planned, however, much to Holmes' detriment: too-curious policemen demanded to be allowed to first investigate the ruins of the boarded-up hotel. Holmes, noticeably alarmed, immediately balked.

When he finally relented, promising to return to the police station later, after having "attended to business affairs," he simply fled, first heading to Texas to try, once again unsuccessfully, to lay claim to Minnie Williams' estate. He was rebuffed by Texas authorities, who demanded to know the cause of Mrs. Williams' death, and were highly dubious of honoring such a claim minus the findings of a legitimate inquest. Holmes' luck was running out.

His capacity to act intelligently wasn't at its peak, either. In Texas, in a panic to flee the ever-increasing suspicion of the authorities whom he had incited in the first place with his abrupt appearance as the "husband" of Minnie Williams, he committed an egregious blunder, one that was eventually to lead him straight to the waiting gallows, and eternal infamy. He stole a horse in Texas, a state that, at the time, often strung horse thieves by their necks until dead. It was a fate that would, inevitably face Holmes sooner or later. He fled Texas to Missouri, where he was apprehended in St. Louis on an unrelated crime.

He was sent to jail awaiting trial, and made the acquaintance, while there, of the notorious train robber Marion Hedgepeth. He inquired to his new-found friend about securing the services of a crooked lawyer, for which Mr. Hedgepeth was offered a sum of five hundred dollars.

Overjoyed, Hedgepeth wrote a letter to his own lawyer, Jeptha D. Howe, who in short order arranged bail for Holmes (who gave the St. Louis authorities a false name), and awaited his next set of instructions.

Benjamin Pitezel, a confederate of Holmes who was assistant on many of his private financial scams, had agreed to go to Philadelphia, under the pretence of opening a patent office, and shortly after, was found dead on his back porch with a badly-burned face. The circumstances of his death were such that the coroner became immediately suspicious at the way the scene had been carefully set-up to make it seem as if Pitezel had self-immolated while lighting his pipe too close to a bottle of flammable chemical.

Obviously, the very notion of that as a plausible means of death was exceedingly peculiar.

It only took a proper examination of the corpse to ascertain that Pitezel had been poisoned. However, other than the suggestion that the luckless man had committed suicide, the coroner could find no evidence of actual crime, and so was forced to rule the death an accident.

At the same time as this was occurring, lawyer Jeptha D. Howe came forward in Philadelphia, ostensibly representing the widow of the dead man. The insurance company, rightfully mindful of fraud, pursued another angle – they wrote to the only known client of the Pitezel Patent Office: Dr. Harry Howard Holmes, of Chicago, Illinois.

It did not take Holmes long to make his way to Philadelphia, with one of Pitezel's young children in tow, to identify the body and claim the insurance money. Mrs. Pitezel, herself, was privy to the scam, and had been assured that a dead body would be obtained to substitute for her husband. Then the money would be collected, divided evenly, and all would live happily ever after.

Alas, her illusions were to be short-lived.

Holmes collected the money, and took fourteen-year-old Ben Pitezel with him.

It was at this point that Hedgepeth, realizing that he had, essentially, been conned by Holmes, confessed to the police all that he knew concerning the man with whom he'd made the five hundred dollar deal. A detective named Frank Geyer, fascinated with the tangled doings of the nefarious, ubiquitous "H. H. Holmes," began to rapidly trail the man backward, to his state of origins, where he discovered not only that the name H. H. Holmes was simply an alias for Herman Mudgett, but that the sinister man's parents still resided in the family house, and thought very well of their handsome son, who had bamboozled them for years with far-fetched tales of making his living as an "inventor."

It was from the family that he finally tracked Holmes to Boston, where he was with Benjamin Pitezel's wife, but with none of his children. In short order they were both arrested, and Geyer began to sweat a stoic Holmes through relentless interrogation.

Geyer gave Holmes a choice of either returning to Philadelphia with him, or being sent back to Texas to hang for horse thievery. Holmes, predictably chose the former, and when once comfortably stationed in his new, private cell, began to prevaricate with gay abandon.

He at first insisted that Pitezel was in South America, and that the body the police had found was simply a cadaver stolen from a morgue, a nod at his old days of "body-switcher" insurance scams.

When Geyer found that unlikely, he then claimed that Pitezel had become despondent, killed himself, and that Holmes had burned the remains in an attempt to make it look like an accident, and collect the insurance.

One great matter distressing Geyer was the fate of the missing Pitezel children, whom Holmes had taken virtually hostage and whom, it was known had been separated and dragged across country on Holmes' bizarre itinerary of fraud and murder.

Geyer first tracked down, after much arduous legwork, a house in Indianapolis that Holmes had rented under a fictitious name. It was here, in an old stove, that young Howard Pitezel had been disposed of cruelly, after he had outlived his usefulness to Holmes.

All that remained were ashes, a partial skull ,and a few bits of bone.

It was in Toronto, though, where Holmes had taken the two young Pitezel twins, that Geyer discovered, with horror, what had been their unhappy fate.

The Pitezel children had been locked inside a great steamer trunk by the diabolical Holmes, who had then attached a hose to the gas jet, asphyxiating the little twins, and thus ridding himself of the inconvenience of their care.

When confronted with this discovery, Holmes replied with faux outrage, exclaiming, "It was a foul deed! What scoundrel did it?"

By the time it all, finally, erupted into national news, Holmes (or rather Mudgett) had fast-become the most despised murderer in American history, up until that point. A score of penny-dreadful pulp publications followed, including the terribly titled book *Sold to Satan, Holmes!: A Poor Wife's Sad Story,* which became an instant, immediate success.

It was largely, however, a piece of utter fiction.

The Holmes-Pitezel story, and the resultant revelations concerning the macabre "Murder Castle" catapulted Herman Webster Mudgett into a strange sort of celebrity, the likes of which America had not yet known: The Celebrity Psychopath. Nearly eighty years before Charles Manson first entered world consciousness as a particularly photogenic rogue, Dr. "H. H. Holmes" would become the first ever sordid tabloid sensation. Some must have wondered what had become of society.

Holmes, not to be outdone, managed to pen his own volume, a largely self-exculpatory piece replete with dissembling, half-truths, and outright balderdash. His more honest attempt at biography came shortly after his conviction, when he called a press conference in his cell, and began confessing to a mind-boggling panorama of felonies and murders.

Meanwhile, Detective Geyer and his men had proceeded to the condemned remains of Holmes former "Castle," where, descending to the basement, they began to excavate in the reeking damp. Sure enough, in short order, they found what amounted to the fragmented, skeletal remains of nearly two hundred victims. The sheer, staggering magnitude of Holmes' crimes paled the hardened policemen.

Holmes confessed, at the end of his life, to having become "a moral idiot." Indeed, it was only after being confronted with the overwhelming evidence of his guilt that the futility of lying gave way to the utter joy he quite clearly exhibited in recounting his grave misdeeds for various reporters and alienists. They, in turn, were only too delighted to have the inside scoop of the foulest murderer any of them had ever encountered in their careers as journalists.

And, they were genuinely dismayed when Holmes' confessions were cut short by his appointment with the hangman.

He had only managed to confess as far as his twenty-seventh victim.

Otto Johann Hoch

Everyone knows the story of Bluebeard, that fairy tale ogre who marries a beautiful young girl, only to forbid her from ever entering a certain room in the castle. When he leaves one day, she disobeys, and, out of curiosity, enters the room.

To her horror, she discovers the bodies of all the women that Bluebeard had previously married to murder for their money, and hide them away. Of course, the implicit horror of that tale lies in the fact that the young woman will soon be the next body to be hidden away by the homicidal husband.

A gruesome little tale to be sure, and, like most legends, it has basis in fact. There have been numerous cases of men (and women) who have married a string of husbands and wives merely to knock them off, usually with some financial motive. The women are frequently referred to as "Black Widows" in the criminal literature, and the men are, predictably called "Bluebeards."

One such "Bluebeard" was Otto Johann Hoch, a German immigrant, born in 1855, under the name John Schmitt. Although facts about his life are vague and hard to come by, what is known of Hoch is that he was one of America's earliest and most prolific of killers, marrying and then slaying an estimated fifty women (although police sources could only credit him with fifteen).

News accounts of the crime were sensationalistic, but what could be ascertained about him was that he had married one Catherine Ramb legally, sired three children, and then abandoned them, taking off for Wheeling, West Virginia, where he married Caroline Hoch. Three months later Caroline Hoch was dead, and her husband (who had been seen administering a poison to her by an unsuspecting reverend who had been called to her bedside), cleaned her out financially, as well as collecting a (for the time) huge life insurance policy. He then made it appear as if he had committed suicide by flinging himself into the river, and disappeared.

He surfaced in Chicago, working in the corrupt meat-packing industry, and continuing his habit of marrying and killing lonely women, the names of which he pulled directly from the Lonely Hearts columns of local papers. All was going well for him, it would appear, until in 1898, he was convicted of defrauding a furniture salesman and sentenced to a year in jail. Digging into the background of Mr. Hoch, a detective named Shippy became curious about the bigamous felon, and, after receiving a letter from the same pastor who had attended the death bed of Caroline Hoch, he also began to suspect Otto Hoch of murder. But he had no hard evidence.

An exhumation of Caroline Hoch's body revealed that all of her vital organs had been removed, so there was no possibility of testing, with the primitive state of medical science at the time, for poisoning. Still, Detective Shippy vowed to continue his investigation.

He would be tracking Hoch for years. The man was released from jail and continued to marry, kill his wives, and make off with the life savings and loot. He felt safe in doing this, as he often changed his name, and, at the time, the embalming fluid used by most morticians was so full of arsenic that not finding traces of arsenic poison was thought to be nearly impossible.

He had moved on to Marie Walcker, marrying and killing her in 1904, before then proposing, almost immediately to her sister (!). The clueless sister accepted the proposal, married Hoch, and then acted surprised when he absconded with seven hundred dollars of her money.

She quickly alerted authorities (perhaps the first intelligent thing she had done in the whole situation), and they just as quickly called in for an autopsy on her sister's body. Owing to the fact that she had not yet been embalmed, the coroner found the tell-tale traces of arsenic poisoning, and they quickly sent the word out to the papers that they were in desperate search for the killer Hoch.

"Henry Bartels," a man who had checked into a New York rooming house before proposing marriage to the landlady twenty minutes later, was identified as Hoch, and the police quickly claimed their man. Mr. Hoch was carrying several revolvers, a passel of wedding rings, and a pen filled with arsenic among his personal possessions.

The resultant media circus had Hoch dubbed the "Stockyard Bluebeard," and the old man certainly seemed to be enjoying the limelight. His demeanor in court was of one who couldn't seem to quite take the proceedings seriously, and there are reports of him whistling and twiddling his thumbs during the trial. It was probably just as well, as Hoch didn't stand a prayer against the amount of evidence against him.

He was sentenced to hang. He did so, protesting his innocence, on February 23, 1906. Interestingly, and nearly thirty years later, an old house that had once been rented to Hoch was found to have human remains hidden inside the walls. The remains were never identified, and the exact total number of victims of Johan Otto Hoch will, most likely, never be known.

Leopold and Loeb

It was an age that "roared."

It was an age when, to be young, rich, and good-looking, meant that society, not as cynical as it has become in recent decades, afforded you an amount of respect and trust associated with your station in life. It was an age when comic book and pulp fiction heroes were, frequently, the Bruce Wayne type of millionaire playboy, who fought crime at night and read the papers in an ascot and smoking jacket during the day.

Society generally associated great wealth and intelligence with respectability and moral courage.

Leopold and Loeb came along to disabuse many of that notion.

***

Nathan Leopold was born with a 200 I.Q. to fabulously wealthy parents who never understood him. As a boy, he was diagnosed with a number of bizarre internal ailments, which rendered him a small, sickly child. He was also sexually molested by a governess, and then became the pederastic paramour of his next-door neighbor's boy, Richard Loeb. It was to be a romantic partnership that would bear sinister, fateful fruit.

Nathan Leopold never liked girls, so to cure him of this malady his parents insisted on enrolling him in an all-girls school, a plan that was to have disastrous consequences. Needless to say, it did little to cure him of the femininity which embarrassed his family. Of course, Nathan did work hard to compensate his masculine shortcomings: He was an expert ornithologist, was fluent in nine languages, had toured Europe, and had graduated from the University of Chicago at the age of eighteen with a degree in philosophy. It would be to philosophy that the wealthy young man would turn to afford him a sort of comfort from his terminal sexual malaise.

He devoured the words of iconoclastic German philosopher Nietzsche, and saw in his work the promise of a New Ideal: an "ubermensch," or a "superman" that would be born from the loins of the elite, and would go on to pioneer a brave new world of beautiful, asexual creatures who would develop great technology, fly to the moon, explore the stars, etc.

Of course, to join him in this world, Nathan Leopold populated his fantasies with big, handsome, masterful brutes. Like his lover, Richard Loeb.

***

Richard Loeb did not leave the world in a good way.

He told the punk to meet him in the prison showers. Richard had had his eye on this particular kid for awhile, and, what with his pull at the prison, now seemed as good a time as any to play his juice card.

He locked the door behind them as they went in, brandishing a razor and saying, "Get your clothes off before I start in on you."

Richard had, by this time, already stepped out of his prison blues. The punk followed him into the shower, taking off his clothes slowly. Suddenly, he turned, kicking Richard in the groin.

The two of them grappled, Richard losing control of the blade and letting it slip from his fingers. The two naked men tussled under the hot spray, and Richard found his blade again, slashing out at the punk with a poorly-aimed fury. He came inches away from slashing his opponent, but somehow the punk managed to wrestle the blade back out of Richard's fingers. This would be Loeb's fatal mistake.

The punk began to slash at Richard, until both men were covered in Richard's blood. The punk would later say:

> After what seemed like several minutes of fighting under the shower, he sank into a sitting position, and in a funny way used two fingers of the right hand to push in some of the flesh of the abdomen, which was cut open.

> I turned to leave the shower. He started to get up. His eyes were big and staring. He lunged at me with everything he had. His hands were clenched like claws. I slashed at him some more and kept slashing until he fell mumbling.
>
> I turned off the hot water. Turning on some cold, I stepped under the shower to wash off the blood. My whole body was red. I left the shower and wiped the water out of my hair and eyes. I heard laughter or a groan. Loeb stood straight up. He lunged at me and knocked me down. His body slipped over me and fell by the door.
>
> He got up and fumbled with the key. He ran out to the dining room tunnel. I did not see him after that.

Loeb had fifty-six separate wounds, and was found lying in a pool of blood in the prison corridor. He was taken to the prison hospital, where his parents rushed to be with him. After lingering for a short while, he said, "I think I'm going to make it."

Then he died. His lover, Nathan Leopold, was by his side.

***

Leopold and Loeb fit each other like a pair of gloves. They were both lovers, (Richard taking the superior role) they were both rich, they were both bored, and they were both intelligent and arrogant enough to believe in their own innate superiority. The constant reading of Nietzsche helped. Together, they set about on a series of small crimes, at first just for the thrill, but later with a more coldly calculating philosophy driving their actions.

Leopold, the more sexually amorous of the duo, was desperate for the romantic attentions of Richard Loeb, who, fancying himself a criminal mastermind, found his own arousal chiefly excited by the prospect of committing a string of random, petty crimes. To that end, he refused Leopold sex until the younger, smaller man agreed to sign a pact that they would embark, as self-appointed "supermen," on a criminal career. Being that he believed himself to be "beyond good and evil," the young ornithologist readily agreed.

The duo set out on a course of arson, vandalism, filing false leads, crooked gambling, and other prankish misadventures, each time upping the ante just a little, each new crime providing just the correct amount of shock and titillation to make their lovemaking that much more intense.

But, of course, as in the case with every such criminal partnership, the thrills soon fade, and it becomes necessary to go to greater and greater lengths to get the same sort of intense charge out of the various acts committed. Loeb fancied himself a criminal mastermind, and chief among his sordid fantasies of mystery and detection was how one might commit the perfect…murder.

The two homicidal rich kids began to plan, intricately, how they were going to kidnap, hold for ransom, and then murder a random individual. They had no fixed target (except, perhaps, what would commonly be referred to today as a "soft target," or, in other words, someone who wouldn't be hard to kill), but they meticulously had the details worked out. Richard Loeb had stolen a typewriter from his fraternity house with the express purpose of writing the ransom notes, each of them opened phony bank accounts, they created false identities to rent a car, and for several weeks traveled to Michigan City, Indiana, just to practice throwing boxes off a train at a certain spot…a spot where they intended to drop a body.

They thought that they could leave nothing to chance. They took to heart Nietzsche's dictum that: "The superman is not liable for anything that he may do, except for the one crime that it may be possible for him to commit – to make a mistake."

The two Supermen did not intend to make a mistake.

Karma, sometimes, has other ideas in mind.

***

There was some confusion as to who, exactly, was going to be their sacrificial victim. At first, they thought they might kill Loeb's younger brother Tommy, but this plan was rejected after careful consideration. How on earth were they to collect the ten-thousand-dollar ransom from Loeb's own family without anyone getting suspicious? Next, they settled on a few boys a little less close to home, one of them the grandson of the president of Sears Roebuck.

But none of the victims they considered, ultimately, seemed like wise choices after they were turned over in the minds of the young killers. They were ultimately rejected. The duo, by this time, had obtained rope, a chisel with black tape around the handle, and hydrochloric acid to blot out the features of their victim, whoever it might turn out to be.

They thought for a short time it might be a young Mr. Rubel, a fellow student with whom they had lunch on an almost daily basis. But it was thought that his millionaire father, a notorious skinflint, would balk at paying the ransom.

The pair searched around desperately for an appropriate victim. Down the street from where Richard lived, was the Harvard Preparatory School, a place ideally suited for two maniacs wishing to lurk young children. The first boy whom these two hooligans spotted while trolling in their rented car was a young kid named Levinson. Levinson seemed like a good prospect, and the two might have been salivating as Leopold sat in the front and Loeb in the back.

"Do we know his address, Nate?"

"Not a clue, Babe."

"Let's see if we can fish it out. He looks pretty contented playing here. I'm sure he'll still be here when we get back."

The two went to a local drugstore to look up the boy's address. Fortunately for the young Levinson boy, he was gone by the time Leopold and Loeb pulled up to the Harvard Preparatory School playground, and the two were, again, out a victim.

That was when the fateful meeting transpired.

The homicidal duo spotted young Bobbie Franks. He was fourteen, not at all physically intimidating, and looked to be an easy mark. He was standing on the corner of Ellis Avenue with some of his chums.

Nathan drove up, and Richard, amicably enough, called out to the boy from the backseat, "Hey Bobbie! Long time no see. Have you been practicing your tennis? I got this new racket I want you to see."

Richard Loeb, in fact, had played tennis with Bobbie Franks a few times, had always been excited by the young boy, had lusted after him. Now, it seemed like heaven (or rather, in this case, hell) had dropped the young lad right into Richard's lap. He could feel himself stiffen in excitement.

Bobby walked over to the car, leaned into the backseat window, and said, "Oh, Mr. Loeb! Hey, I didn't know it was you. Jeepers, you had me scared half to death for a minute."

Richard said, smirking, "Yeah, I guess I might have, Bobbie. Anyway, I was wondering if you wanted to come along with us for a ride, check out my new tennis racket. It's a real beaut."

Bobbie looked back over to his friends, some of whom seemed to have strolled away in boredom. The rest of them seemed to be more interested in the candy of the soda fountain window than what he was doing. He still wanted to hang out and play.

Besides, he wasn't too sure about these guys. He knew Richard Loeb, of course; their families moved in the same circles. And weren't they distantly related somehow? He wasn't sure. At any rate, he told them:

"No, no I don't think so Mr. Loeb."

Richard felt himself grow tense.

"Aw, come on Bobbie. Say, if you go with us, might be a soda and some candy at the end of the ride for you. And, man, I tell you, you are gonna want to see this racket. It's a real beaut. Ain't that so, Nate?"

Leopold nodded his head in front, said, "Sure thing, Richard. Best-looking racket I've ever seen. Amazing piece of equipment."

Bobbie looked up and down the street again chewing his gum, said, "Well, okay, I guess if it don't take too long. But I gotta be home in time for supper, okay?"

"Sure, gotcha! Nathan, step on it! Bobby, this here is my good friend, Nathan. No, you go ahead and sit in the front by Nathan. I like stretching out my legs while I ride."

Bobbie Franks got in the car. It would be the last mistake of his short, tragic life.

Richard Loeb picked up the chisel he had brought for just this purpose.

He struck Bobby in the back of the head.

Four vicious blows.

The boy slumped over.

Nathan Leopold continued to drive.

Richard crawled over into the front seat of the spacious luxury car, stuffed rags in the mortally-wounded boy's mouth, and wrapped him in an old robe. He was bleeding profusely.

"Oh, God, I didn't know it would be like this!" Leopold said, his voice querulous, somewhere between tears and hysteria. He continued to drive through heavy traffic, with Bobbie Franks dying on the floor of the car. They drove twenty miles, stopping to have sandwiches for dinner, and so that Leopold could call home, to tell his father he would be getting in late.

It was at the Panhandle Tracks of 118th Street, that they stopped. It was now dark, and darkness would provide the cover they needed to do their grisly work. Loeb unloaded the body, using the acid to permanently disfigure the features of the corpse. Then, Richard smuggled the body from the car to a culvert, wearing his hip boots to wade in the muck. He shoved the body into a drainage pipe. This was where Richard made *his* fatal mistake that night.

They stopped on the way back for another meal.

Then their plans really went into action.

It was time to start the blackmail part of Operation Superman.

They first burned Bobby's clothes, and the robe that was stained with his blood. Next they drove to Indiana to bury everything else he was carrying that could not be burned, such as his class pins.

While they were in Indiana, they typed out the ransom note that would be sent to Bobbie's parents. After that, it was back to Chicago to place a phone call.

"Your boy is being held for ransom. He is safe and unharmed. Tell the police and he will be killed at once. You will receive a ransom note with instructions tomorrow."

Loeb, using the name "George Johnson," sent a note detailing to Mr. Franks that he was to give them ten thousand dollars in twenty- and fifty-dollar denominations, in an old cigar box, wrapped in tissue paper, and sealed with ceiling wax. He was instructed that the way to deliver this money would be sent by instructions after one p.m.

Leopold and Loeb celebrated that night by drinking and playing cards till dawn. Then, taking the rental car to Leopold's garage, they furiously worked trying to clean the bloodstains out of the upholstery, telling the Leopold chauffeur Englund that they had been driving while drinking some "wine," and that it was simply a nasty spill.

He would later testify against them.

Then, Richard Loeb took his typewriter and drove it to a vacant lot abutting a swamp, where he tossed the keys of the typewriter in. He then took the typewriter itself, and tossed it away in another swamp.

Next, he took a train to Indiana, where he left a note for Bobbie Franks' father in an envelope in the telegram slot. It gave further instructions for Mr. Franks, but, on the whole, it was a rather pointless effort on Richard's part.

His victim had already been found.

A foot was seen by a passing brakeman, sticking out of the drainage pipe. It was no time before the youthful body was identified.

A massive manhunt followed, perhaps the biggest manhunt in Chicago history up until that point. Nathan Leopold was finding it hard not to be paranoid, but Richard on the other hand, was relishing the shock waves the crime sent through the media and the city.

One could argue that, at this point, Richard was acting on some deep-seated impulse to be found out. Perhaps it was an urge for the ultimate publicity, a superman-like immortality, that was driving him, but he began to make himself a pest to the investigating officers, informing them, in his own amateur sleuth fashion, of little pet theories as to who the actual culprits in the killing could be.

At one point, Richard even told them that: "That's just the sort of cocky little sonofabitch I would choose if I were going to kill someone." He really would have been better off just keeping his mouth shut and laying low, because it was after this statement that the detectives began to suspect that their amiable, wealthy young pest knew a lot more about the crime than he was able to glean through simple amateur deduction.

Soon, the secrets of Leopold and Loeb began to unravel. The typewriter and keys were found; a pair of glasses that had slipped out of Nathan's pocket that night were also found. When checked against the records of the store where they were purchased, it turned out that only three pairs had been sold in all of Chicago...one pair to Nathan Leopold.

Now the police had their prime suspect.

Leopold protested that he had lost the glasses while out on one of his ornithology trips, but the police weren't buying it, and continued to hammer at him.

"He was a nice little boy. What motive did I have for killing him? I didn't need the money; my father is rich. Whenever I want money all I have to do is ask for it. And I earn money myself teaching ornithology."

***

Nathan Leopold told the police that on the night of the Franks murder, he and Richard had been out with a couple of girls. The cops weren't convinced. Two reporters earned themselves a Pulitzer by breaking the case open wide.

They obtained letters that Richard Loeb had typed, written on the same stolen typewriter with which he had hammered out the ransom note to the Franks. The letters matched perfectly, and this seemed to seal the fate of the two "fun time" killers.

Of course, it was going to be difficult to find someone to represent the legal interests of the loathsome duo, and that responsibility finally fell to the single most famous lawyer of the age, Mr. Clarence Darrow, who delivered a closing argument in the case that is still much studied by legal students.

In his closing argument, Darrow stated:

> They pull the dead boy into the back seat, and wrap him in a blanket, and this funeral car starts on its route.
>
> If ever any death car went over the same route or the same kind of a route driven by sane people, I have never heard of it, and I fancy no one else has ever heard of it.
>
> This car is driven for twenty miles. First down through thickly populated streets, where everyone knew the boys and their families, and had known them for years, till they come to The Midway Boulevard, and then take the main line of a street which is traveled more than any other street on the south side except in the loop, among automobiles that can scarcely go along on account of the number, straight down The Midway through the regular route of Jackson Park, Nathan Leopold driving this car, and Dick Loeb on the back seat, and the dead boy with him.
>
> The slightest accident, the slightest misfortune, a bit of curiosity, an arrest for speeding, anything would bring destruction. They go down The Midway, through the park, meeting hundreds of machines, in sight of thousands of eyes, with this dead boy.
>
> For what? For nothing! The mad acts of the fool in King Lear is the only thing I know of that compares with it. And yet doctors will swear that it is a sane act. They know better.

In the end, Darrow's impassioned defense mitigated the death sentences awaiting young Leopold and Loeb. The two were convicted and given life sentences. In prison, due to the influence of their families, they lived like little kings.

They were instantly reunited at Northern Illinois Penitentiary, given large cells with furnishings, books, and toilet amenities that other prisoner's didn't enjoy. They also washed and ate their meals in the officer's mess. Their meals were of better fare than the typical prison food, and altogether, one supposes Leopold and Loeb could not have enjoyed any better situation behind bars.

Of course, in the end, this did very little to help Richard Loeb, whose amorous tendencies proved to be his ultimate undoing. As for Nathan Leopold, he was paroled in March of 1958. By 1961, he had married a widow and become a laboratory technician in Puerto Rico. His book, *Life Plus 99 Years*, became a best seller.

Still, he claimed that the awful act that he had committed so many years previously continued to burn in his consciousness, and would do so until the day he died.

He died August 30th, 1971.

John Dillinger

John Dillinger was, by all accounts, a good boy. Young, athletic, the son of a German immigrant grocer, John was known for being a quiet boy and a good student.

It was in sixth grade that young Johnnie Dillinger made his first "heist": stealing coal.

The magistrate took one look at the defiant young man in his courtroom, idly chewing gum, and said, "Mr. Dillinger, you must remove that gum from your mouth this instant!"

Only wishing to be helpful, young Johnnie did as he was requested. He promptly took the gum from his mouth and stuck it on the bill of his cap, causing the judge to explode.

"Your mind is crippled!" he cried.

But, crippled or not, it was still a dangerous mind, and would become more so as the young boy grew into adulthood.

***

There is very little to account for the criminal course that young John Dillinger set out upon in life. By all accounts, his home life was good, and he even got on well with his father's second wife, Elizabeth. During the first part of his life, it is said that he rarely caused his parents any trouble (save, perhaps, for the aforementioned coal theft incident), but all of that changed when Dillinger Sr. decided to sell his grocery and buy a farm in Moorseville. Young Johnnie detested farm life, and so decided that he would make his living working as a machinist part-time. He outright refused to help his father work the land, a situation that would stick in the craw of Dillinger Senior for many years to come.

When he wasn't zooming around on his motorbike or working in the machine shop, Johnnie was pursuing a whole new interest in life: the seedy underworld of pool halls and "sharks." He spent a lot of time at Big John Gebhardt's dive in Martinsville, usually losing to the hustlers, but always turning up again to lay down a couple of more bucks to flush down the drain. This was the beginning of his education in the world of hoodlums and thugs.

A more wholesome interest of young Johnnie's was baseball, and he joined a local team, proving to be an excellent player, and attracting the attention of his second-cousin, Francis Thornton, whom he quickly began dating. Johnnie must have loved Francis, because he quickly decided she was going to be the woman he was going to marry.

Her father, however, would have none of it, and in a day and age before people were liberated to do as they please, his refusal to offer up the hand of his daughter was final. Johnnie quickly became bitter over the whole affair, and started taking treks to Indianapolis, seeking to drown his romantic sorrows in the loving embrace of various prostitutes.

It was at this time that he first contracted venereal disease.

Something greater than gonorrhea must have been eating at the young man's mind, however, because on the night of July 21st, 1923, he impulsively stole his first car, taking it for a joyride and later abandoning it. Maybe he didn't understand why he had done it, but the terror of possibly being discovered and sent to jail finally drove John to join the Navy to avoid possible prosecution.

Here, as fireman third-class Dillinger, he was assigned to the U.S.S. *Utah*, and shipped out, only to prove an incorrigible, lousy sailor who was in the brig more often than he was out of it. He finally jumped ship permanently and was listed as a deserter, with the first-ever bounty of fifty bucks being placed on his head.

Back in Indianapolis, he continued to date and dream of a way to make himself a great man in the world. On his own terms, of course.

He married briefly, but spent little time thinking about his wife. Instead, he felt the ever-present allure of baseball and the pool hall calling him. It was at Gebhardt's where he would launch his first foray into outright armed robbery.

***

The men huddled around a table, playing cards.

"He takes the receipts out every Saturday night. I know the route he takes, right out in front of the church. Couple of gunsels to help me, and we could take him easy. He's an old man; probably doesn't have much fight left in him."

"I'm out. I can't take the heat. I'm already on parole." The third man laid down his cards, picked up his cigarette, and glanced out the window nervously.

Johnnie Dillinger, however, was made of sterner stuff.

"I'm interested, Ed. Let's get this job planned out pretty well in advance, though. I don't like any loose ends."

Ed Singleton was a former con with a number of tall tales and good advice when it came to "pulling heists." Johnnie Dillinger thought he was learning a lot from him. He was up for whatever criminal plans the man wanted to enact.

The first job was to rob grocery clerk Frank Morgan, a sixty-seven-year-old man who had a little more fight in him than what the two hoods had first imagined. They waylaid Morgan outside of the church just as they had planned.

Dillinger smacked him in the side of the head with a bolt wrapped in a rag, and Singleton brandished a gun. Morgan went down but got back up, causing Dillinger to hit him again, and Singleton brought out the gun.

The gun went off by accident.

The two would-be robbers ran, and Mr. Morgan would later require eleven stitches. Although Morgan claimed later he couldn't identify his attackers, the local sheriff felt that he already had Johnnie Dillinger pegged as one of them. Upon taking Morgan out to the Dillinger farm, a tearful John confessed, overcome with sadness that he had attacked an elderly man that he had known since he was a child. John was quickly locked up in the Moorseville County Jail, to await trial.

Dillinger was given bad legal advice. He was advised to plead guilty and "throw himself upon the mercy of the court." Apparently, the court was not feeling merciful on the day of his sentencing, as Dillinger, not yet twenty-three, was sentenced to over ten years in prison. (Ironically, Singleton, his accomplice, received a far more lenient sentence.)

Dillinger was sent to Pendleton, and upon arrival, his first vow to the warden was that he was determined to escape.

"I've heard that kind of talk before," said the Warden.

"Well, I'll go right over the administration building if I have to," said John Dillinger.

His escape attempts became routine.

He once tried to jump a train when he was being escorted back to Pendleton after an escape attempt. Another time, he was found hiding in a laundry while outside his cell. Yet another time, he sawed through the bars of his cell door with a makeshift device. None of these escape attempts amounted to anything, and for what it was worth to Dillinger later, it is probably better for him that they didn't.

It was at Pendleton that he first met the gentleman bank robber Harry Pierpont, a kind of royal duke of crime that was considered to be irresistible to women and also an expert on the ins and outs of banditry. His sidekick, Homer Van Meter, was a tough-talking con who played jester in the high criminal court of fools that was gathering around Pierpont. Both men were only too eager to school young Dillinger in the ways of crime, and the young inmate was eager to learn.

Both Pierpont and Van Meter were considered trouble by the prison staff, and both eventually earned themselves transfers to Michigan City, a much tougher Indiana prison. Dillinger, finding himself alone, and facing a parole hearing, wanted badly to rejoin his criminal compadres.

He therefore devised a plan to get himself transferred to Michigan City,

Noting that one of the members of the parole board (who, at any rate, were determined to deny him an early release) was a man who had once watched him play on his minor league ball team, Dillinger requested to be transferred to Michigan City, as "they had a real team up there."

The man put in a good word for young Dillinger, and the parole board grudgingly obliged.

It was while at Michigan City, reunited with his two senior criminal friends, that Dillinger first met "three-fingered" Jack Hamilton, a con who was doing twenty-five years for stealing a car. Hamilton was an even more seasoned pro when it came to bank heists, and in time, it seemed that young Dillinger knew everything there was to know about robbing banks.

All he lacked now was experience.

***

Johnnie was up for parole in a few short weeks, and the plan was for him to commit a series of small time bank heists until he could get the money and resources together to bust his gang out of Michigan City.

This task he would undertake almost immediately upon parole.

It was 1933, and the Depression had already left many banks failing. After attending his stepmother's funeral (an event at which a sympathetic pastor delivered a sermon aimed directly at Dillinger, a sermon of which he later claimed, "You will never know how much good that sermon has done me."), he quickly gathered together a gang of outlaws and knocked over the bank at New Carlisle, Indiana, getting $10,600.

The plot was almost lost when one of the gang members, William Shaw, was arrested on unrelated charges. Dillinger and his lieutenant happened upon the scene, and throwing the car in reverse, made a hasty get away.

***

It must have been a slow morning at the Commercial Bank of Daleville on July 17th 1933. A man walked into the bank, leveled a gun at teller Margaret Good, and said:

"This is a stick-up, honey."

At first, Margaret didn't know if the man was joking or not, but she decided the gun he was carrying looked real enough. The man, a darned handsome scoundrel in a blue suit and straw hat, ordered everyone into the vault, jumped over the railing, scooped $3,500 into his pocket, and then an accomplice came into the bank, also brandishing a weapon. Later, a thoroughly frightened Miss Good would tell police that he had been, really, rather courteous and kind about the whole affair.

Police were suddenly searching for Dillinger, who had just recently managed to make himself a hot commodity.

Dillinger made his way to Ohio to wait for things to cool down, visiting a new girlfriend, Mary Longnaker. Soon, however, he was back in business, knocking over the National Bank of Montpelier for a $10,110 take. He also managed to lift the bank supervisor's .45 automatic pistol. "This is a good haul," he later said, "and a good gun, too."

Next on the agenda was the Citizens National Bank of Bluffton. Dillinger came in with an accomplice dressed in an expensive gray suit and straw cap, leveled a gun at the book keeper, told him, "This is a stick-up," and proceeded to rifle through the cashier's drawer.

When not satisfied with the small amount of money he was getting, Dillinger said, "There's more money in this here jug. Let me into the vault!"

Suddenly, an alarm went off, and Dillinger's accomplices ran into the bank shouting it was time to lam. Dillinger ignored them, still carefully stuffing money into his bag while the two men who were with him went outside and fired guns into the air. The police were on their way, and Dillinger was forced out and into the getaway car before he got any more than a measly three thousand. (Which all things considered, was really a rather princely sum for that day and age.)

Next on the itinerary was the Massachusetts Avenues State Bank in Indianapolis. This was a momentous heist for Dillinger, who took everything here he could lay his hands on, and made off with an enormous amount of money. With it, he would be able to finance the jailbreak of his criminal cohorts Pierpont and Van Meter.

In what must have seemed like a plot twist from a dime novel, Dillinger hired an Italian thread maker to fill a barrel headed toward Michigan City prison with guns, and then mark the barrel with a huge red X. The cons quickly got word of the scheme, secreted the guns away in their cells, and used them to enact the largest prison break in Indiana history. Overnight, the legend of the Dillinger gang was born.

But Dillinger himself was to run into trouble only a short time later. While visiting his girlfriend in Dayton, police detective Russell K. Pfauhl got wind of the fact that Dillinger was to be in town. He managed to waylay the gangster while he was standing in his girlfriend's living room, looking at pictures of their trip to Coney Island.

So it was off to an Ohio jail cell for Dillinger, and what was to be the most daring escape yet in the history of his criminal career.

***

Dillinger was playing cards when his gang (whose escape from prison he had engineered) came to break him out of prison.

"John, your gang has come for you," said the fellow he was playing cards with. John realized that this was, unbelievably, the truth. His time in prison was at an end.

For days, Dillinger had been going on about the fact that his gang was going to come and rescue him. In this notion, he was not to be disappointed.

The scene played out like this:

Sheriff Jess Sarber was relaxing with his wife and deputy after dinner reading the papers, when Pierpont and two accomplices walked in the door. He looked up from what he was doing, leaned across his desk, and said, pleasantly enough, "What can I do for you gentleman?"

He had no idea, but gentlemen, he wasn't addressing.

"We're officers from Michigan City. We want to talk to the prisoner John Dillinger."

Sarber sat there, plainly unconvinced. His wife was reading the paper, and his deputy was working a crossword. Sarber said, "That's fine, but first I need to see some credentials."

Suddenly, one of the men got angry with the conversation. He pulled out his gun, said, "These are our credentials!"

Sarber pushed the gun away limply, as if trying to ward off the impending shot.

Oh, you can't do that," he said.

Pierpont was having none of it. Sarber went for his gun, and was shot once in the gut, once in the hip.

Sheriff Sarber went down.

"Go and get the keys to the cells!" Pierpont demanded to the unbelieving two witnesses. As Sheriff Sarber tried to rise on his elbow, Pierpont dealt him a duo of vicious blows that opened his head.

"I'll do as you say," said Mrs. Sarber. "Please, just don't hurt him anymore!"

She ran to get the keys.

The Terror Gang strode into the cells and found their man. He turned to the fellow he had been playing cards with and said, "Hey, want to come?"

"No thanks," was the curt reply.

The Terror Gang heard many prisoners call after them as they went, imploring them to release them, too. They resisted the impulse, realizing they would suffer a mob scene if they did so.

"Just wait till we are gone. Then if you want, you guys can just walk out!" one of them is reported to have said.

On the way out, Dillinger saw Sarber laying in a bloody pool, and bent down low over him. Sarber was a good sort, Dillinger figured, as far as lawman were concerned, and he turned an accusatory eye toward Pierpont and asked, "Was this really necessary?"

Pierpont is reported to have not responded to Dillinger's question.

As the gang was leaving, Sarber was reported to have said, "Men, why did you have to do this to me?" He then turned to his wife and said, "Mother, I believe I'm going to have to leave you." He then died.

The Terror Gang was already out the jail door and into a waiting getaway car. Their first stop after the jailbreak was Indianapolis, where gang molls Evelyn "Billie" Frechette and Mary Kinder were waiting. The gang's plans soon revolved around a series of daring bank heists. Their first order of business though was to rob the police armory in Peru, Indiana, where they made off with enough weaponry (including grenades, gas masks, and bullet proof vests) to arm a small island nation.

The new Dillinger Gang (a name Pierpont encouraged, as he thought the name Dillinger had a better ring to it) made their base of operations in Chicago, living in apartments on the Northeast side. Indiana State Police Inspector Matt Leach became the gang's most ardent law enforcement menace at this point, so that the members of the gang dared not even drink hard liquor lest the indefatigable Leach catch them with their pants down, napping.

Apocryphal stories surround the feud between the desperadoes and the avenging lawman, but a few of them (most circulated by reporters and a few by Leach himself) have Dillinger telephoning Leach with various threats and sending him copies of an old leaflet called, "How to Be A Detective." None of this actually happened, most researchers believe, and Leach's stories to the press concerning an incipient leadership squabble between Pierpont and Dillinger seem to have been entirely bogus.

In reality, John Dillinger was the undisputed leader of the gang, and the marauders had greater worries on their minds.

Their first big bank job was going to be planned with the precision of a fine science.

***

To enact what they would come to think of as the "foolproof" method of robbing banks, the Dillinger Gang would come to rely on the method perfected by German bank robber Herbert K. Lamm, a man who had once served under the Kaiser's army during World War 1.

Lamm had immigrated to the United States and began a series of bank robberies until his arrest in 1917. His method included first "casing" the bank, making a detailed floor plan, having his fellow gangsters rehearse their parts as if it were a theatre production, and giving an allotted amount of time for the job, making sure that all of his men were out the door and gone once the allotted time had expired.

With this German efficiency, Lamm had managed to be very successful as a bank robber. At least for a short while.

Pierpont and Dillinger knew the system, and also had a pretty good idea of the first bank they were going to hit with it: the Central National Bank in Greencastle.

It was on October 23, 1933 that they made their move.

***

The Studebaker was running outside with Clark behind the wheel. Dillinger, along with Pierpont and Mackley, went inside, with Hamilton left out front, acting as a "tiger" determined to shoo anyone off that should attempt to come into the bank while they were robbing it.

"Get your hands up and keep 'em where we can see 'em! We aren't advertising!"

Dillinger jumped over a rail into the cages, and started to scoop cash into his bag. Mackley stood by the door, timing it all, making sure they could be done in the amount of time allotted. According to plan, they shouldn't take one more minute than was necessary. But the Boss had already cased this joint days before, and everything seemed like it was going by plan.

"Hurry up you mucks! Time is ticking!"

An old lady, obviously a foreigner, started to walk out the front door before Mackley grabbed her by the arm.

"Hey, where do you think you're going? Better get back inside lady!"

She turned to him and snorted angrily, "I go to Penny's, and you go to hell!"

And he let her go.

John looked over the counter at a passel of money laying there. In front of it, an old farmer stood with a terrified look on his seamed old face. He had his hands up like all the rest.

John asked him, "Is that your money, or the bank's money?"

The old farmer looked nervously at the pile of dough and said, "It's my money."

John said, "Well, you keep it, okay? We're only after the bank's money."

And that was that. This was how a legend of John Dillinger came to be born.

The total take for the Terror Gang was $73,346. They waltzed out of town on country roads, missing every police roadblock, and getting away without a single shot being fired.

Matt Leach began to tell more stories concerning the apocryphal phone calls that Dillinger was supposedly making to him, claiming that Dillinger would call him up and scream at Leach that he was a "stuttering bastard." Whether this was true or not (the calls, that is) Leach must have hoped that he could inflate the Dillinger ego to a point that it would prove the bandit's own undoing.

He was very nearly right. When Dillinger found himself suffering from a rare skin ailment, he thought to get medical treatment from a doctor by the name of Charles Eye. An ex-member of the gang informed Chicago police that Dillinger was going for treatment, and the Dillinger Squad thought to lay a trap for the seemingly unstoppable gangster.

Dillinger, while driving his favorite car, and having his girl Billy Frechette in the seat beside him, sniffed out that something was afoul as soon as he pulled up to the doctor's office. He quickly sped off, and found himself being chased by a cordon of police cars.

Dillinger, leading a merry, quasi-comic chase through Irving Park, often narrowly missing other cars and pedestrians, managed to shake all the cop cars on his tail except for one driven by Sergeant John Artery and his partner Art Keller.

Getting in beside the Hudson Terraplane, Keller leaned out the passenger side window and began pumping shotgun shells into Dillinger's car.

"Hey! Someone is shooting at you, honey!" said Billie Frechette.

Dillinger smiled, the very picture of calm, and floored the accelerator, leaving their pursuers in the dust. Dillinger shot down a side street, causing Artery to overshoot the mark and go spinning down the road. By the time he got back to where Dillinger had turned off, he and Billie had long since disappeared.

"That bird can sure drive!" Art Keller was quoted later.

***

The informant was eventually paid off by Dillinger, and the gang set their sights on relocating to Wisconsin, specifically Milwaukee. It was here that they robbed the bank at Racine.

Pierpont went in that day with a huge Red Cross poster, completely confusing the tellers when he hung the poster over the large picture window looking out. The tellers, though, could have been no less surprised when Dillinger and gang member Mackley came in, produced weapons, and said, "This is a stick up!"

Initially, the tellers thought it was a joke, but were soon disabused of the notion. Everyone was commanded to get down on the floor as Dillinger went behind the cages and began raiding.

Unfortunately for the bandits, someone had managed to trip a secret alarm that rang at the police station, and it was no time before a car was dispatched to see what was going on. The officers who answered the call took their time, as the alarm was prone to go off by accident. They just assumed that this was another false alarm.

They were freed of that notion as soon as they entered the bank, and Pierpont managed to disarm both of them, although not quickly enough for the liking of Mackley.

Mackley shot one of the police officers, a man named Hansen.

By this time, a crowd was developing outside, and the gangsters realized they had a problem.

"I've got it all! Let's beat!"

Dillinger and the other crooks pushed a passel of women out the front door as human shields, and were met with a barrage of gunfire from across the street. Law enforcement were firing on them, but they were aiming high to avoid hitting bystanders.

Realizing quickly that leaving through the front was not going to be an option, they hustled out the back of the bank to a waiting car, taking with them the bank president and a teller by the name of Mrs. Patzke.

They drove quickly through back roads, finally letting off their terrified hostages, but not before John asked Mrs. Patzke if she might be interested in becoming the cook for the gang.

"Some other time," she said.

The gang spent that winter lounging in Florida, where they had rented several cottages by the water. It was here that they could kick back and relax, eat meals prepared by gang molls Billy Frechette and

Mary Kinder, and plan their next move. Life must have seemed good, if somewhat tense.

They left Daytona Beach for Tucson, Arizona. Along the way, the gang – or some gang – robbed the First National Bank of East Chicago, Indiana, and an officer was killed. Although Dillinger always denied responsibility, the police hung the crime on the shoulders of the Dillinger gang.

In Tucson, a fire broke out in a hotel in which the gang was staying, and the firemen who rescued the gang's luggage for them grew suspicious, opening the suitcases full of weapons. It seemed as if luck had finally run out for the seemingly unstoppable Dillinger gang.

Quickly rounded up, the gang was split up with Mackley, Pierpont, and Clark sent to Ohio to stand trial for the killing of Sheriff Sarber, and Dillinger himself going to Crown Point Jail in Indiana to stand trial for the East Chicago bank robbery he always claimed he had no responsibility for.

Crown Point Jail was supposed to be escape-proof.

But John Dillinger proved that where there is a will there is a way.

***

Vigilante squads patrolled outside the prison gates, as they were well-aware that Dillinger had escaped from prison before. The situation this time was, however, markedly different: All the rest of the Dillinger Gang were in jail. Dillinger, if he was going to try and make a break for it, was going to have to go it alone.

He did just that.

Using a razor wire from a boot strap, Dillinger managed to carve for himself a wooden gun, which he disguised with shoe polish and which looked good enough to convince Deputy Sheriff Ernest Blunk that it was an actual gun.

It was only a short matter of time before Dillinger had rounded up a dozen guards, and with the aid of a black convict named Herbert Youngblood, had commandeered an escape car, taking deputy Sheriff Blunk and an auto mechanic along with him as hostages.

He let them go after a short while, giving them each four dollars and apologizing that that was "all he could spare." He crossed state lines into

Illinois, and the Federals quickly entered the manhunt. They assumed that Dillinger would be headed toward Chicago. They assumed wrong.

He instead went to St. Paul, a city that had built a reputation for its crooked law enforcement agency that, essentially, made their city a safe haven for traveling gangsters wanting to "cool down." There he joined the two gun molls Billie Frechette and Mary Kinder, as well as the newly-paroled Homer Van Meter, who had resumed his criminal career almost immediately upon release.

Other members of this new Dillinger Gang included John Hamilton, who had served under Dillinger before, Tommy Carroll, Eddie Green, and the psychotic Lester Gillis, who was better known as "Baby Face Nelson," a ruthless and cold-blooded killer who had served with Al Capone and Bugs Moran, and who was a veteran at both bootlegging and robbing banks.

Dillinger was in a hurry to make a quick amount of cash, as was Nelson. Dillinger was also eager to help Mackley, Pierpont, and Clark out of their jam, as they were all three currently awaiting trial for the Sarber killing. All of this seemed like an uphill struggle for the desperately wanted gangster, and, to make matters worse, Van Meter and the psychopathic Nelson did not get on well at all, often having to be separated before their heated arguments came to blows, or worse.

They struck a bank in Sioux Falls South Dakota, a job in which a jubilant Baby Face jumped atop a desk at the bank and blew a policeman away while he was standing outside the window.

"I got one of them! I got one of them!" he squealed in delight.

This was not the way that John Dillinger wanted to operate. It had only been three days since he had broken free from the supposedly escape-proof Crown Point Jail.

Tommy Carroll had the entire police force of Sioux Falls under the muzzle of his machine gun, lined up on one side of the street outside the bank, while thousands of spectators looked on excitedly. Dillinger and the others hustled out of the bank with the loot, and got into the getaway car. The citizenry, for the most part, believed that they were watching the filming of a new gangster epic, a rumor that had been carefully spread by Homer Van Meter several days earlier when he had blown into town posing as a Hollywood producer!

Dillinger was careful to spread a carpet of roofing nails on the road behind them as they made their escape, counting on blown out tires to give them some more time. Their take from the job was $49,000.

If Nelson had managed to mar the good, clean record of John Dillinger (as far as bank robberies were concerned) with the Sioux Falls job, then the next job they did, a bank in Mason City Iowa, was a comic opera episode in which everything went disastrously wrong from the get go.

To begin with, the bank president, upon seeing Homer Van Meter enter with a gun, completely lost his nerve and locked himself in his office. Van Meter, knowing that the keys to the vault were in the president's office, began to fire through the door. A guard standing in a cage above the lobby fired a tear gas shell into the center of Eddie Green's back. Green spun around and released a volley of machine gun fire at the guard. A woman leapt out of the bank door with one shoe on, ran down the alley, and told Baby Face Nelson that he needed to alert someone that the bank was being held up.

Dillinger stood outside and collected hostages. Someone shot at him from a third-story window. On instinct, Dillinger spun around and returned fire. The man who shot at him was able to duck to safety just in time.

Inside the bank, a testy teller was doling out stacks of one-dollar bills to an increasingly impatient John Hamilton. Hamilton could not open the vault (the keys still being in the cowering bank president's office) and this was the best he could do.

"Open up this damn door!"

"I can't. I don't have the key! All I can do is pass the money through the bars like we're doing!"

The teller was being very slow doling out the stacks of money.

Dillinger sent Van Meter in to tell Hamilton that the job was botched, and it was time to go.

"No! It's hell to leave all that money!"

"C'mon!"

There was still about $200,000 left in the vault. The gang got away with about $52,000 dollars in small bills.

Shipley, the man that had initially fired on Dillinger from a third-story window across the street, fired again. Dillinger and the rest of the gang piled into a waiting Buick that was loaded down with hostages clinging to the running boards.

For fun, Baby Face shot one of them in the leg and watched him drop off as they sped away.

"Did you have to do that?" screamed Dillinger, now thoroughly disgusted with Nelson.

Nelson is supposed to have shrugged Dillinger's anger off.

***

"I should have killed that man," brooded Hamilton later, while a doctor was treating his and Dillinger's small wounds. The doctor would have called the police, but was certain that if he did, he would have been killed.

The gang had made their escape from the Mason City job slowly, their car packed with hostages on all sides, and Nelson getting out of the car at intervals to fire volleys of machine gun fire. The cops gave up the chase, unwilling to risk the lives of the hostages. The hostages were all eventually freed.

As for the three men that Dillinger hoped to free in Ohio, Makley, Pierpont, and Clark, two of them (Pierpont and Makley) were condemned to die in the electric chair for the killing of Sheriff Sarber, and the third, Clark, was given a life sentence. Dillinger failed to do anything to free these men, although precautions around the prison they were being held at were extremely tight in anticipation of a raid by Dillinger to free his compadres.

Meanwhile, Dillinger was posing as a "Carl Hellman" in St. Paul, living in an apartment with Billy Frechette and Homer Van Meter. Two FBI agents, Nalls and Coulter, found out the location, and went to pay them a visit. While Billy Frechette stalled them at the door, she gave John time to get his machine gun. Just then, as luck would have it, Homer Van Meter was coming up the stairs. When one of the agents asked Van Meter what he was doing there, he impudently replied that he was a soap salesman, and told the FBI agents that he could prove it if one of them came down to his car to view his samples.

As soon as Van Meter got downstairs to the front door of the apartment building, he whirled on the FBI agent, pulling his gun and telling him "You asked for it, so I'll give it to you!"

The terrified agent rushed past Van Meter and went out the door. Van Meter followed close behind, commandeered a salesman's horse and wagon (!), and galloped off like an Old West desperado.

Dillinger and Frechette went down a back exit, but not before John thought to spray the hallway with bullets. The FBI man outside the door returned fire, and Dillinger was wounded in the leg. The couple got away in the nick of time, but where to go now?

First Dillinger arranged with a lawyer to have certain monies secreted away in the inevitability of his taking a "long trip." Then, he and Van Meter robbed the police station in Warsaw, Indiana, taking a small arsenal with them. This last move was a very bold one, even by Dillinger standards.

The gang settled at a remote fishing resort in Wisconsin called Little Bohemia. For them, it was to be a sort of last hurrah, and for the FBI it would become a monumental embarrassment, but whatever the case, it would begin the end for John Dillinger and his bank-robbing days.

The gang was holed up in several little cottages in Little Bohemia. The FBI, under the direction of Chicago head Melvin Purvis, convened a raid on the place in the middle of the night.

Right away, the tense G-men managed to fire on three innocent tourists leaving a cottage, killing one and wounding two more. The gunfire, of course, immediately alerted the gangsters sleeping in nearby cottages.

Baby Face Nelson, always ready for a fight, slipped out of his cottage and exchanged fire with the FBI before running back inside.

The gang escaped in separate vehicles: Dillinger, Van Meter, and Hamilton all escaping in one car, Nelson in another (he later killed an FBI agent at another resort) which he drove to Chicago, and Tommy Carroll heading to Michigan. The gang's women were left to cower in a basement as FBI guns battered the cabins until morning, the agents assuming that the gangsters were still hiding inside.

***

The FBI put out a $10,000 reward and a shoot-to-kill order on Dillinger. They were mightily embarrassed by the Little Bohemia raid, in which one of their agents and an innocent man had been killed, and they were more determined than ever now to finally stop Dillinger by any means necessary.

Several states where Dillinger had robbed banks joined in the $10,000 reward. It seemed to be only a matter of time before Dillinger would find himself at the end of his thirteen-month spree.

Many men who bore a resemblance to Dillinger (who, in turn, often bore a striking resemblance to hardboiled screen star Humphrey Bogart) found themselves in danger during the next few months. Dillinger himself only managed to turn up at a chicken dinner at his father's house in Indiana in May of 1934. He announced to his father that he wouldn't have to worry about him anymore, as he was going away on a "long trip."

***

Detective Sergeant Martin Zarkovich had a plan.

He could deliver Dillinger into the hands of the police with the help of his friend Anna Sage, a whorehouse madam from Germany. The only condition was that Dillinger was to be killed instead of captured. It was this last condition that caused Chicago Police Captain John Stege to reject the offer, stating, "I'd even give John Dillinger a chance to surrender."

Chicago FBI head Melvin Purvis had no such compunctions, however, and agreed that he would stop deportation proceedings against Sage (who became the infamous "Woman in Red" to history) if, indeed, they could deliver up a dead Dillinger.

It was thus on July 22nd, 1934, that Anna Sage led a young man named James Lawrence out of the Biograph Theatre in Chicago into a waiting ambush, where he was gunned down by Martin Zarkovich. Immediately, FBI press releases announced that they had finally succeeded in killing John Dillinger.

***

There is some dispute about whether "James Lawrence" really was John Dillinger. For the purposes of this volume, the various strange theories about this are not really worth going into. This author believes that the man who was killed outside the Biograph Theatre that night was, in fact, John Dillinger. Other authors, including *Bloodletters and Badmen* author Jay Robert Nash, believe differently. The idea of a conspiracy or mystery in the final fate of John Dillinger is used to bizarre, comic effect in the mammoth science fiction novel *The Illuminatus Trilogy* by Robert Anton Wilson and Robert Shea.

It is perhaps more instructive to note that Dillinger died an ignoble death, ambushed and shot down in an alley like an animal, in cold blood, betrayed by a woman he trusted.

As for the various members of his gang:

> Tommy Carroll was killed by policemen June 5th of that year.
>
> Eddie Green was killed April 3rd.
>
> Homer Van Meter died in a shoot out with police that year. The date was August 23.
>
> After being wounded in a fight with police, John Hamilton was never seen alive again. (He is believed to have been buried by fellow criminals in an abandoned lot.)
>
> Mackley was killed trying to escape from prison, September of '34.
>
> Pierpont went to the electric chair in October of 1934, almost jubilantly.

In the words of a then-popular radio personality The Shadow: "Crime does *not* pay."

Truly…

The Mad Butcher of Kingsbury Run

Two small boys were racing through a desolate section of Cleveland known as "Kingsbury Run," a desolate wasteland of heaped garbage, old cars, and shanty houses frequented by hoboes, and skirted the top of a local ravine popularly referred to as "Jackass Hill." One of the boys turned to his friend, said:

"Hey, what is that down there?"

His friend looked down the steep embankment, shading his eyes from the sun. "Looks like some feller probably passed out drunk."

The other boy did not think so. He carefully made his way to the brush at the bottom of the ravine, with his friend following at his heels more cautiously.

Down there, among the brambles and the bushes of the ugly, pitted wasteland of the Run, the boys spied a scene that sent them running in terror.

The two boys had found two bodies, both of them decapitated, exsanguinated, and washed. One of the bodies showed evidence of having been doused with acid, while another quite clearly had been unceremoniously scorched during an attempted cremation. Both bodies were missing their penises.

The men showed signs of rope burns on their wrists, thus indicating that they had been bound and decapitated while alive.

The identity of one body was ascertained to be that of Edward Andrassy. Andrassy, the son of Hungarian immigrants, already had a nasty reputation at the age of twenty-eight. He had served some small time in a penal colony, was known as a womanizer, was a suspected homosexual (a fact that would later interest investigators as a possible motive), and had been rumored to have been in altercations, variously, with Chinese gangsters, Italian mobsters, and a husband whose wife he had sodomized under the pretext of curing her of her "female troubles." In short (and adding to this the fact that he was a known alcoholic and an occasional dealer in pornography) there was no short list of suspects that might want him dead.

As to the identity of the older man found with him, it was never ascertained.

The police didn't connect it at the time, but a year earlier, the lower half of a woman's torso had washed up on the shores of Lake Erie, near an amusement park. She had been severed at the knees, and the odd discoloration of the skin suggested that the body had been treated with some chemical agent, perhaps in an effort to eradicate it. Several weeks earlier, the upper portion of this victim had washed ashore thirty miles away, but it took awhile for the man who discovered it to realize, exactly, what it was. She became known as "The Lady of the Lake," and the rest of her body was never recovered.

To this day, she remains unidentified.

***

Cleveland, at this period in her history, was a swarming haven for vice, a breeding ground for illicit activities that gangsters and other assorted felons found quite to their liking. To counter this perceived crime wave, a "no nonsense" mayor named Harold Burton was elected on the promise that he would "clean up the city."

His first order of business was to contact famed "Untouchable" lawman Eliot Ness, whose agents had managed to help topple the empire of Al Capone and would go on to inspire a famous television program. Ness proved to be the man most right for the job, and quickly set about reorganizing the police academy and fire departments, as well as making a number of lightening strikes against local gambling operations.

Ness was an outstanding success at his job, but all of his crime fighting acumen couldn't prevent the next in the puzzling series of murders that would go on to spread terror throughout the city.

It was January 26 when the killer left another of his astounding calling cards.

Butcher Charles Paige called to inform the police that an anonymous woman had alerted him that there was a body laying in an alley near his building. He claimed that, upon investigation, he found these facts to be correct.

This time, the body (or rather, the torso) was placed in a basket, with additional body parts wrapped in burlap sacks and underwear being wrapped in newspapers. The remains consisted of the torso, thighs and "right upper extremity" of a woman later identified by fingerprints as prostitute Flo Polilo, age 42. The coroner noted that the flesh seemed as if it had been expertly cut.

Detectives May and Musil ferreted out the sad details of Flo Polilo's final days, in hopes of ascertaining who might possibly be responsible for committing such heinous acts upon her person.

Flo had once been married to a good man, a mail carrier who seemed to genuinely care for her. Unfortunately, she let booze get the better of her, and in the late 20s, she went on the skids, moving to Cleveland to "straighten herself out." But instead, she fell in with a rat's nest of scum alley personalities: pimps, hookers, gamblers, bootleggers… She knew the dregs, and apparently enjoyed their company.

Everyone reportedly liked Flo, but the very nature of her life left the list of suspects to her killing pretty long; after all, figured the cops, if you lay down with dogs, don't be surprised if you get fleas.

It was February 7, 1936 when the rest of Flo was found behind an abandoned house, apparently an upper torso and thorax that proved conclusively that Flo had died from…decapitation, while alive. The body was amazingly well preserved due to the bitter cold.

The police now had three decapitation deaths in a year and a half period. Still, they were too short-sighted to connect the shocking murders to one man. The mind boggles.

***

The Republican National Convention was held in June of 1936, and the delegates were in the city by Friday the 5th for schmoozing and boozing. Eliot Ness was personally responsible for the security, and handled a grueling schedule of planning and preparation. He was now the "boy wonder" cop of the city, and he had earned the respect of Mayor Burton with his ceaseless raids on underworld establishments and gambling.

The delegates to the convention must have been very impressed with all the new construction, as the centerpiece of Cleveland construction was an immense mall that included Public Square, the Terminal Tower (the largest building in the world at the time), and a host of restaurants and shops to please the tourists.

Not far from this sparkling new construction, however, was a vast industrial wasteland that was the underbelly of the city. Crisscrossed by train tracks, covered in belched soot and bleeding out a refuse of unemployed men and drunken vagrants, this area was fifty blocks from the architectural showpiece that had just been constructed.

It was two boys, yet again, who discovered the next victim, on their way to go fishing. Making their way through Kingsbury Run, they spied what they took to be a pair of pants rolled up. One stout kick however, revealed a severed head.

The boys, both panicked, ran back home to call the police. The police wasted no time in making their way to Kingsbury Run, and finding the head, soon set about looking for the rest of the victim. They found the body, ironically enough, in some bushes in front of the railroad police station. The body had been exsanguinated, washed clean, and unceremoniously dumped in front of the station in what appeared to be a "cat and mouse" fashion.

The police already realized that the man (known only as the "Tattooed Man" because of the six distinctive tattoos he sported), must have been killed somewhere else. There was simply no way the killer, whoever he was, would have been able to drain the blood and clean the body in the area of Kingsbury Run. The coroner confirmed one thing for them: Decapitation had been the cause of death. It was almost a repeat of the murders of Andrassy and the unidentified first victim.

Eliot Ness soon found himself thoroughly fascinated by the prospect that there was a psychotic killer loose in Cleveland decapitating people, and met with the head of the Homicide Division to personally discuss the cases.

Ness came to the conclusion that the elusive head chopper was one man, despite the fact that there were important differences in the M.O. as far as the male and female victims were concerned (in example, the female victims were mutilated as well as decapitated), and he gave instructions that there was to be no further info from the police during the convention and absolutely no suggestion that they were looking for a single killer.

Ness, as far as he was concerned, was done with the case after this brief consultation. His first responsibility, he thought, was in dealing with whatever corruption he found lurking in the bowels of the police department. He left the investigation of the decapitation murders up to Detective Hogan, who wore out his shoe leather in a futile attempt to identify the latest victim, the "Tattooed Man." That particular avenue lead nowhere, and even the seven million visitors to the Great Lakes Expo were unable to come up with a positive identification of this individual after being shown a death mask and other photographs as part of the "War on Crime" exhibit.

The fifth victim, who was discovered July 22nd of 1936, was found near a hobo camp on the southwest side of the city, decapitated, in an advanced state of decomposition, with his head wrapped in clothing not far away. Police estimated he had been lying there some two months, and also noted that the killer had altered his M.O., having obviously killed the vagrant on the spot (the police found a massive quantity of dried blood under the body) and simply left him there, not bothering to remove it to the Kingsbury Run location.

Nearby, a pile of filthy old clothing, presumably the victim's, was found bundled.

The media ran with the story of the latest killing, and sensational headlines began to crop up in the papers, turning the unknown killer into a menacing mystery man. The police, while trying to quash the publicity, were not having much luck doing so; soon a period of panic began to settle over the city as people became afraid of becoming the next victim.

That next victim was found by a hobo floating, in two sections, in a shallow creek. Additional pieces of flesh were found by police, as well as two legs and a thigh once the small creek had been dragged by grappling hooks. Bloody clothing was found wadded in newspaper, as well as a bloodstained hat.

This latest murder drew massive attention and a crowd of onlookers, and the police realized that they were now held hostage to public scrutiny as far as the Kingsbury Run killer was concerned. The head of this victim was never found, and he remains unidentified.

A passel of twenty detectives was assigned to the case, many of them going undercover as hobos or homosexuals, haunting gay bars and bath houses in hopes of ferreting out the killer. Also, for the first time, they began to comb the records of insane asylums for recent discharges, thinking that the killer might be found among them. Alas, it was to no avail.

Meanwhile, Ness was perturbed that he had to drop his graft investigation and devote attention to the Mad Butcher. He instructed his detectives to follow every lead, even absurd ones, and gradually a feeling of menacing fear began to settle over the city as newspapers blared forth sensationalistic prose concerning the doings of the degenerate fiend.

Everyone, it seemed, became suspect, but most especially butchers or anyone who might be seen carrying a large package or walking, for any reason, with a knife in their pocket. The Federal Narcotics Commission theorized that it was the work of a wild pothead, as "loco weed cigarettes" were known to drive people to insanity, but Ness himself knew that, in all probability, they were facing a criminal of an unusual caliber. After conferring with fellow policeman and coroners, he managed to draw up a profile of the elusive butcher.

For starters, Ness felt that they were dealing with one man, and that this man was probably heavily built, muscular, and had a good working knowledge of human anatomy. Whether or not he was a doctor was strictly a matter of conjecture, as it was felt that even a hunter could recognize anatomical features sufficiently to enact the expert decapitation that the victims evidenced.

It was also felt that the killer had a private residence where he could commence the perpetration of his deeds, as the decapitation killings were quite messy; police felt that this might be a doctor's office or even a butcher shop, but could also be just an ordinary residence that the killer (who so far preyed exclusively on the lowest social classes) might use to lure his victims with promises of work or food.

Ness likewise felt that killer was apt at putting on his "mask of sanity;" he was obviously a man who could go about the streets and mingle with average society without arousing too much suspicion. Although Ness didn't know it at the time, he was painting a portrait that would become all too familiar to law enforcement in the coming decades: a portrait of a sociopathic serial killer.

***

The addition of Detective Peter Merylo to the case was, felt Ness, a step in the right direction.

Merylo was an eccentric cop who made a name for himself by arresting homosexuals after they left the gay bars together (homosexuality was illegal in Cleveland at the time). Merylo was, by all accounts, a short, stocky man with a fierce temper and a tenacity that often netted him results, and so he seemed perfect to head up the Kingsbury Run investigation. He had, in fact, been fighting to be put on the case when Ness finally relented.

His methods, however, remained unorthodox, one example being his parading up and down the Run in his long johns in an effort to "bait" the Mad Butcher. Inevitably, this unorthodox cop got the lion's share of weird witnesses and suspects to interrogate, which included (but we're sure was not limited to): a man that liked to masturbate over dead chickens, a "voodoo priest," a man with a "death ray," and other assorted loonies. It got to where, based on Merylo's offhand pronouncements to the press, the public came to see him as the official mouthpiece for the Mad Butcher investigation, which was decidedly not true.

The rest of the force thought that Ness was using Merylo as a mere distraction away from the bogged down investigation.

Victim seven was found February 23rd, 1937, washed up on the beach of 156th Street. It was a body missing a head and arms, one that had been dead two to four days, and had been in the water three. The only other information they were able to glean post-mortem was that she was approximately 25-30 years old, lived in the city, and had once been pregnant. Unlike the other victims, oddly, she did not seem to have died due to decapitation, the head seeming to have been removed after death this time. Her legs had been taken off at the knees with a sharp blade, and the upper portion of her torso was found floating, two months later, in another location, closer to the mouth of the Cuyahoga River. To this day, her identity has never been ascertained.

The coroner felt positive by now that the killings were the work of one sexual psychopath, albeit one that was unique in that he chose to abduct and kill both men and women. The missing limbs, he felt, allowed the killer to more easily transport the bodies, and also, to help foil any attempts to identify the remains. The coroner also felt that the killer was obviously anatomically adept, and that they should be looking for a surgeon or medical student – or perhaps even a butcher.

The profile was a striking example of forensic investigation, but, much to the chagrin of the coroner, Ness had the papers quash it, in an effort to avoid the carnival-like atmosphere that sensationalism brought to the case. Ness was tired of his detectives following up worthless leads, and he was determined not to let the public get any more whipped up into a frenzy than they already were.

Unfortunately, this quashing of the coroner's report did little to endear the public safety director to the coroner's office, and started an interdepartmental feud that doubtless did little to help solve the baffling crime.

Victim eight was found June 6th, 1937, by a teenager who had been watching Coast Guard boats off the Cuyahoga River. Coming home underneath a bridge, he spotted a rotten burlap bag that contained the rotted remains of a tiny woman, as well as a newspaper from 1936.

After examination, the remains were found to have been treated with quicklime, and the mouth contained an impressive amount of dental work. The coroner firmly believed the victim to be an African American, and there was some dispute over whether or not the remains were those of a missing prostitute named Rose Wallace.

According to the coroner's report there was "considerable hacking and cutting of the 3rd, 4th and 5th cervical vertebrae, but it was impossible to tell from the skeleton whether decapitation was the cause of death."

It was not long after this that another body was found floating in the Cuyahoga River. A floating torso with thighs from which all the abdominal organs had been removed. The entire body, sans head, was recovered. This victim, like so many others, was never identified.

The police, while trying to maintain a tight gag on publicity, were busily going about investigating local medics and physicians, as it was now generally acknowledged that the killer, whoever he was, was a reasonably skilled anatomist. They focused on doctors, specifically those who they felt might have a predilection for perversion, or who might be closet homosexuals.

One of their chief suspects, a Dr. Francis Sweeney, seemed to fit the profile they were looking for all too well: He was a violent drunk who had managed to lose his position at a nearby hospital because of his profligate ways, and he was rumored to also be bisexual. He had, likewise, grown up in the area of Kingsbury Run and had had an office there at one point.

Dr. Sweeney was also a first cousin with Congressman Martin Sweeney, a harsh critic of Cleveland mayor Burton and Eliot Ness, whom he accused of chasing phantoms of corruption within the police department while maniacs like the Mad Butcher roamed free. Sweeney the Congressman railed that Ness should be "sent back to Washington."

Three more bodies turned up in 1937. That same year, riots broke out in the city over labor strikes, and the Ohio National Guard was called in, ready and willing to crack skulls. They did exactly that, and hundreds were injured, as the city descended into maelstrom over economic turmoil and panic caused, partly, by the escalating violence of the Mad Butcher.

Finally, what seemed to be a possible lead in the case cracked a couple of hours away in Sandusky, where a human leg had been found by a dog. A Detective Cowles was dispatched to Sandusky to see if he could ferret out whether or not this leg had any connection to the spate of decapitation homicides.

While it was eventually ascertained that the leg was simply medical refuse, Cowles did remember that Dr. Sweeney, an early suspect in the Mad Butcher case, had been eliminated because of an alibi that he was always in Sandusky, drying out at the veteran's hospital, when the murders presumably went down. After doing some asking around the hospital, and learning that patients such as Dr. Sweeney were free to come and go as they pleased, Cowels felt himself grow excited; he began to think of Sweeney as a very important suspect again.

Cowles found an inmate named Archaki, who was serving out his sentence at the Ohio Penitentiary Honor Farm, a facility that abutted the Sandusky hospital where Dr. Sweeney was frequently a patient. The good doctor was kept in liquor by Archaki, while Archaki was kept in phony scripts. Archaki was convinced that Sweeney was, indeed, the Cleveland Torso Killer.

He related how he had met Sweeney several years earlier in a bar, and how Sweeney had asked him a number of uncomfortable questions, as if he was sizing up his potential as a victim. Archaki noted that the bodies of the victims were always found when Sweeney had "disappeared" from the Sandusky institution for a few days.

Although the leg turned out to have no connection to the Mad Butcher killings, Cowles came back to Cleveland agitating for a "discreet" investigation of Sweeney. It had to be discreet because of Sweeney's family ties to the hostile politician.

On April 8th 1938, a single leg was fished out of the Cuyahoga River. A month later, two burlap sacks containing the bisected torso of a mutilated woman were also claimed from the river. The head and hands were never found, and the woman remains unidentified.

Meanwhile, Ness was feeling the pressure to find the culprit. He was well aware that any investigation of Sweeney, if it was not handled "discreetly" could blow up in his face. It would be assumed by the press that Ness was simply having Sweeney tailed because his first cousin was a politician with a fiery temper who had castigated the lawman publicly. Nevertheless, Sweeney was now the number one suspect, and a detective was put on his heels to track him constantly. The police soon learned that Sweeney had a bizarre sense of humor, as he enjoyed leading the cops tailing him on a merry chase through seedy bars and department stores. He even introduced himself to the lead detective, and suggested, since they were going to be spending so much time together, that they should get to know each other better.

Ness resumed his activities searching out corruption and trying to modernize the Cleveland police. He kept a wary eye on the investigation, but refused to become too personally involved. However, he found that the Mad Butcher slayings were the story that just wouldn't die, as an accidental discovery of two bodies, a male and a female, were found at a local dump on East Ninth Street. The head and hands, however, were both found with the female victim, the remains (bones) of the male victim being discovered some hundred yards away. The skull of the male victim was found in an old soup can.

The investigators had their doubts about this being the work of the Mad Butcher, but the Cleveland citizenry had no doubt that it was.

Ness responded to the public pressure in the worst possible way: by organizing a heavy-handed raid on the hobo camp at Kingsbury Run. Arresting dozens of men and burning their shanties to the grounds only led to condemnation by the local press for Ness' "cruel" actions, and, though the hobo camps were carefully searched, it led to not a single sliver of evidence that was useful in the investigation.

Ness found himself backed into a corner; public pressure was mounting, and with his career hanging in the balance, he hastily decided to commence with an interrogation of their chief suspect, Dr. Francis Sweeney.

The interrogation was done in a swank hotel suite, after Sweeney had been given a few days to dry out. Secrecy was maintained out of deference to Sweeney's family connections. Also, although the police were certain that they were on the right trail, it behooved them to keep the interrogation under wraps to preserve what little reputation Dr. Sweeney had left; just in case it was found that, indeed, he was innocent.

Ness was on hand in the room, and a polygraph was administered. Sweeney was asked, point-blank, if he was the culprit they were looking for. After answering in the negative, his results were carefully scrutinized by an expert.

Once examining the polygraph results, the lawmen all found they agreed on one thing. Dr. Francis Sweeney was, indeed, the Cleveland Torso Killer.

At one point, Ness sat in the hotel room with Sweeney, perched at the edge of a bed, and eyed him warily. Sweeney paced the room, becoming more and more agitated as time dragged by.

"Well, are you satisfied?" he asked.

"Yes," said Ness. "I think that you're the killer."

Sweeney reacted angrily at the suggestion, and bent low to Ness' face, saying, with his fists balled at his hips, "Oh, you think, huh? Well, prove it!"

Ness then recounts that he got off the bed and went into the next room to get his confederates. To his horror, he found that the other officers there to interrogate Sweeney with him had decided to go out for coffee! Ness went back into the next room, where he said the terrifying Sweeny found the situation amusing.

"It looks like your buddies decided to skip out on you Ness!"

Ness hurriedly got on the phone and reached his partners, suggesting that they get back to the hotel room, pronto.

Ness had Sweeney tested again on the polygraph. The results were much the same: The lawmen were satisfied that they had their killer.

The problem now was that there was nothing but circumstantial evidence to back their case. Ness felt certain that a conviction was out of his reach, and the idea of constantly tailing the wily Sweeney seemed out of the question, too.

In the end, Dr. Sweeney, if he was the killer, may have taken himself out of commission. He spent the years from 1938 until his death in 1961 in and out of a variety of state mental hospitals and veterans' homes. He was always a voluntary patient, and could sign himself out at any time that he liked (although the Sandusky Veteran's Hospital had a note on his record that, in the event that he should sign himself out, the police were to be notified immediately).

The last ten years of his life, from 1955 on, were spent in a mental hospital in Dayton. He was confined there by court order, and spent his leisure time sending odd postcards to Eliot Ness and others. Perhaps mocking the lawman on his inability to "get the goods" on his chief suspect.

No one was ever tried officially for the Cleveland Torso Killings. The bodies of victims eleven and twelve were found in mid-August of 1938. Some august personages have suggested Torso (Sweeney?) as a possible culprit in the killing of Elizabeth Short, the aspiring Hollywood actress who has become known to history as the "Black Dahlia," and whose mutilated torso was found in L.A. in 1947. Although there are a number of striking similarities in the killings perpetrated by the Cleveland Torso Killer and the killing of Elizabeth Short, the sheer geographical distance between Ohio and California makes this seem, we feel, unlikely.

However, it is not for us to weigh the evidence of such claims. The reader is invited to investigate the truth for him- or herself.

William Heirens

The young boy liked to look through peepholes. Keyholes. He was always strange in that way; he seemed to be a natural born little spy.

He had sneaked into the house after realizing that the front door was unlocked. All was quiet inside, and he could hear the floorboards creak as he stepped down the hall toward the back rooms. He had not yet thought about the fact that someone might be there.

Suddenly, he could hear what sounded like moaning down the hall. He crept forward in the darkness, his hands moving along the edge of the wall as he went. He walked to the door from which he could hear the moaning coming out. It sounded like a woman.

He could hear the bed moving.

He could hear a man inside there. What was he doing to the woman? Was it painful?

He put his eye to the keyhole.

He felt his heart begin to race, felt his blood pressure rise, and his breath grew ragged as he looked in wonder through the keyhole.

The man was on top of the woman. She had her legs bent far back, and they seemed to be moving back and forth. They were both starting to make a lot of noise.

The boy leaned forward to get a better look. Suddenly, some change slipped out of his pocket onto the floor. The man jerked his head around, and the boy suddenly thought, with mounting terror, that the man could probably see his single eyeball at the keyhole. He turned and bolted down the hall and out the door as he could hear footsteps thudding across the boards behind the door of the bedroom.

Later, the boy had told his mother what he had done. She did not thrash him, putting his mischievous prank down to the misadventures of a curious youth. She did, however tell him that: "All sex is dirty. Women are dirty. If you touch them, you get a disease."

Little William Heirens already had a disease, however, one that would come to infect the rest of his natural life.

***

A picture of Adolph Hitler was pasted, side by side, with one of Mussolini and one of Goering in the boy's scrapbook. He liked to sit and romanticize about the power exuded by these seemingly titanic personages. He fancied he could feel the chill of evil coming off the photos. They excited something in him primal, deviant; something he did not understand. It was a feeling that was altogether wrong somehow, but delicious and strange at the same time. He often masturbated when he looked at these pictures

He sometimes wore women's undergarments now, which he stole off the wash lines while rambling through lonely backyards, engaging in a little peeping tom routine that also excited him a great deal. These items were as cherished as the talismanic pictures of fascist dictators in his scrapbook; even more so, as they helped transform him, turn him, momentarily (at least in his mind) into that strange opposite that his mother had warned him about.

He liked the smell of them. He liked the way they made him feel; vile and electrified with a sick energy that he could not explain.

He was, he had guessed by this point in his life, markedly different from other men.

***

He began to burglarize houses, at the same time garnering a collection of firearms, one of which he carried with him at all times.

This latter choice first brought him to the attention of the police. They arrested the boy, quickly finding in his house a veritable arsenal of weaponry: a rifle, a .38 caliber pistol, several revolvers. Where he had gotten these items, the police wondered.

They did not wonder long. The boy readily confessed to a string of burglaries and arsons. He was 13 years old.

The judge put him on probation, and he was sent to a private psychiatric institution in Indiana. After a short time there, he transferred back to St. Bede's Academy in Illinois, where he was an excellent student for three years, skipping his first year and enrolling as a sophomore. He had, apparently, a remarkable I.Q. Moreover, after all, if he had made mistakes when he was younger, he had surely learned the error of his ways by now, hadn't he? He was, after all, the son of a prominent and respectable businessperson.

Or so some must have thought.

In truth, William Heirens was simply waiting, brooding, biding his time and perfecting his various schemes and tactics. He fully intended to go back to burglary; the lure of it was too great; the excitement was too tempting to ever really stave off the habit for more than a few years.

Soon, he would have another, more sickening thrill to arouse him.

***

His first victim was 43 year old divorcee Josephine Alice Ross. He had been burglarizing various apartments and warehouses on Chicago's North Side for awhile, but here was the first time he had ever entered a place with a sleeping woman who suddenly awoke.

He must have been making too much noise, because, as he entered the bedroom, he saw that the woman was sitting up with the covers pulled up over her breasts. By the look on her face, he could tell that she was utterly terrified. What if she started screaming or something? He panicked.

He quickly grabbed the knife he had brought along with him.

He slashed her throat from ear to ear.

Blood spurted everywhere.

He found that this, unaccountably, bothered him. He wrapped a bandage around the wound.

No good. Blood was still pouring from the gaping wound. Next he took a red dress he found and started to wrap that around the face. That was a little better. No, he didn't have to look at that offensive wound.

He walked around the apartment in confusion for two hours. Then he left. On the way out, he passed her daughter on the stairs.

It was June 1945.

More would follow.

***

The woman came out of the bathroom with a towel wrapped firmly around her. She took one look in her living room and began screaming. There was an oaf-like intruder going through her purse. She dropped her towel, standing there screaming, and the noise must have sent William's blood coursing through his veins because he suddenly pulled his gun and blasted her twice. She went to the floor, and to finish her off, he got out his knife and stabbed an additional two times, leaving the knife jutting out of the second wound.

But, somehow, the sight of the bloody, naked woman…bothered him, unaccountably. He carried her body into the bathroom, and carefully washed the blood out of the wounds. He then placed towels around the victim's head, and covered her with a housecoat. Then he did something that later, to himself at least, must have seemed strange.

He wrote on the wall in blood:

> For Heaven's sake catch me before I kill more. I cannot control myself.

And he was only being honest.

***

It was January 2nd, 1946, 12:50 a.m., when Suzanne Degnan stirred from sleep.

The six-year-old girl said, "I don't want to get up. I'm sleepy." A neighbor heard Heirens as he gagged the child and took her out the window with him. Before he left, he left a note that said:

> "Get $20,000 Ready and Waite for Word. Bills in 5's and 10's. Do Not Notify FBI or Police. BURN THIS FOR HER SAFETY."

Heirens had no intention of ever returning the child.

***

He took her to an abandoned basement. She struggled against him, but he was quick with his work. He immediately snuffed her life with his powerful hands, and laid the body down in the darkness, gloating over it. Ah, now here was the same sort of powerful thrill he had first felt when he gazed upon his pictures of Hitler, or wore the stolen panties he paraded around in secret. Except, now the feeling was magnified a thousand fold, or ten thousand fold. It was always like this when he killed.

He looked at the little body. So frail, so lifeless. But it would be a problem for him to get it out of here in one piece. He paced nervously about the room, noting that something about the little girl he had just murdered…bothered him. Irritated him. Why couldn't she just get up and walk away? What was this death that he could deliver with such expert deftness and unfailing finality with his own hands? He had to know. He had seen blood. Now, he wanted to know more.

He carefully began to dissect the body.

***

Later, he walked around with a shopping bag full of her body parts, dropping them down the sewer as he went.

***

It was June 26th, 1946, when he was finally captured. A call came in from the janitor of a North side apartment complex that they had a suspicious man on the premises. Officer Tiffan Constant was sent to investigate.

When he got there, he found tenant Mrs. Leonard Pera and the janitor struggling with a man, who soon broke free of their grasp and leveled two shots at the detective. Heirins missed, and the detective did what he could to grapple the youth to the ground.

But Heirens was a tough one to subdue, and it was not until another policemen came on the scene that Heirins was finally cuffed, by dint of having three flower pots broken over his head.

Heirens was taken into police custody, where he was administered truth serum. Unknown to the officers however, Heirins had been injecting HIMSELF with truth serum for a good long time, all the better to build up an immunity to the drug.

It was then that baffled police began to uncover the twisted, knotted mind of William Heirens, and found themselves wondering at the bizarre personality they had happened upon.

When asked if he had been responsible for the death of Suzanne Degnan, Heirins answered that "George did it."

"How did George do it?" asked the police interrogators.

"Well, George was robbing a man's home the night before and saw a ladder across the way leaning against a building."

"When did he kill Suzanne? The next night?"

"George went into the yard."

"What yard?"

"The yard where the little girl was killed."

"Did George do anything else?"

"He placed a ladder against the window and climbed in."

"He climbed in the window?"

"Yes, and then he carried her out. George is a bad boy."

"George Murman" was apparently Heirens alter-ego, a second personality that could commit murder and any other number of foul deeds, and feel no guilt or shame. Most policeman thought that Heirens was probably faking, laying the groundwork for an insanity defense that would come later.

Although there have been many well-documented cases of split-personality, it is an incredibly rare psychiatric condition, and one that sociopaths often turn to when trying to justify or explain away their bizarre acts. In the case of Heirens, it didn't help him much to elude the consequences of his crimes.

He was convicted and sentenced to three life terms. In the comfort of his cell, he no doubt has found sufficient leisure time to stare at pictures of Mussolini and Hitler, speak with "George Murman" (George Mur-der-man. Get it?), and ruminate over his various crimes.

He is currently incarcerated at the Dixon Correctional Center in Dixon, Illinois.

Ed Gein

The lonely little man looked out the filthy window of his farmhouse at a moon that rose up full and fat in the distance. Over the fields, spectral beams of light played against the tall, unkempt grasses as he carefully ladled his pathetic dinner of pork and beans onto a filthy plate, not caring that the meal was bland and unpalatable.

Inside, in the squalid darkness of his home, all was right. Out there, amongst the roughnecks and common folk of his small Wisconsin town, the little man was a non-entity; a loser. He was the local butt of jokes, a sort of makeshift village idiot.

In here, though, within the crumbling walls of this decrepit farmhouse where he had lived since he was a boy, he was safe and secure; even better than that, he was master of his own domain. He ladled the slop of beans into his mouth and considered what he wanted to do for the evening.

The home in which he now sat was obscured by darkness, but even a cursory examination of the contents would reveal a disordered, filthy mess. The kitchen was a nightmare of dirt, piled up books and magazines, rusted cook pots, and general disorder. The rest of the house was falling into a similar state of squalor and disrepair. But what did it matter to the little man? In here, sitting over his can of pork and beans, he was master of a strange kingdom that few would ever wish to trespass upon.

Only one room in the entire house was kept clean, and that was the room of his sainted mother, now long in her grave. The little man made certain that that room was always well cared for, and that it would remain, exactly as she had left it, on the day of her passing.

The little man finished his meal, his eyes still roaming through the filthy darkness. Milky slivers of moonlight illuminated some of the odd treasures he kept around the room, and the sight of these, piled in the darkness, excited the fillip of sensation that seemed to drive him, from the base of his reptilian brain outward, as he planned and plotted his next little excursion.

And, oh, what treasures he had in mind to find tonight!

***

Ed Gein was always a peculiar young man.

He and his brother Henry were both fanatically devoted to their mother, Augusta, who reared both of her sons to be God-fearing Christians, mindful of the evil ways of wine, women, and song. Their father George was not so taken with scripture himself, and was often the focus of his wife's great, righteous anger. It was all the same to Ed when the old man finally up and croaked, leaving the trio of Ed, Augusta, and Henry to tend the 160-acre farm by themselves.

Two strokes, however, left Ed's mother a bedridden wretch, and it was left to Ed to take care of her, his brother Henry having decided that, just perhaps, the world beyond the farmlands of Plainfield, Wisconsin, might hold some promise that he, hitherto, had not contemplated. Mysteriously, Henry died while out hunting with Ed one fine day, trapped in a circle of burning trees.

Ed escaped unscathed.

Folks around those parts always thought that that was mighty peculiar.

Thus, Ed finally had Augusta all to himself. And he was a loyal son, making sure to tend to his mother in her final illness, even as folks around him began to notice that the already strange, feckless Ed seemed to be growing even more peculiar by the day.

He no longer had to work the land, for one thing; a government subsidy provided him ample time to pursue his individual strange hobbies and interests. These included collecting books on anatomy, racy detective magazines, and true accounts of cannibalism throughout the world.

***

The little man walked through the cemetery in silence, spade and shovel in hand. Beneath him, resting in their sepulchral cocoons, generations of Plainfield dead waited for the resurrection promised them in the Book of Revelations, although none of them could have conceived of a resurrection quite like the one the little man had in mind for them. When he broke dirt on the first grave it was the decisive act. He dug deep into the fresh soil, eager to get after his moldering presents. He could possess the flesh then, or what remained of it, and put it to his own use. All the better to conduct his "experiments."

***

Ed, for all his faults, had always been a trusted member of the community. Sure, he might be the occasional butt of jokes, but that was simply a result of his being a little slow, a little strange. Often, neighbors caught him laughing at his own, private jokes, which he was careful never to share with anyone else. A "sleepy eye" didn't help matters much, but Ed was still trusted enough to baby-sit for local children, to do odd jobs, to have over for a supper every once and awhile.

He wouldn't (or so locals thought at the time) harm a fly.

***

After driving the bodies home from the cemetery, under cover of darkness, Ed would hustle his treasures inside the house, where he could quietly work with the fetid remains. Here, he could fashion a playground for his own perverse, fascinated pleasures.

Here, he could cut out the female parts, the parts of the body that really interested him. Ed had always been considered somewhat effeminate, something of a "sissy." What was it about women that was so fascinating to him, so compelling?

Well, at last, he had the body of a female now, to explore the territory between male and female, life and death, and content himself at some level.

***

No one knows why, particularly, Ed picked Mary Hogan as the first of his two victims. Perhaps, it is reckoned, she physically resembled his own mother to the point that Ed felt that he had to possess her, just as he possessed the remains of so many women dug up from the crawling confines of Plainfield Cemetery. Perhaps it was just that her occupation, as a server at a local tavern, offended his inner sense of propriety, drove home the point Augusta Gein had always made to him about whorish women and their evil ways.

***

Whatever the reason, it was after closing up one morning that Eddie stumbled into the tavern in a daze. He may have stood there for a few moments while Hogan questioned him.

"Why, Eddie Gein; what are you doing here at this hour?"

Ed didn't answer. Mary Hogan couldn't have known what strange errand had brought the little man into her bar that morning.

"Hello Mary... I just wanted to drop by and see if you needed any help."

"Help? Ed? Are you out of your mind? Hey, what have you got with you there?"

Ed crept forward from the shadows, suddenly lifting the old .22 rifle and firing one shot into Mary Hogan, who slumped over the bar. He then went about his work quickly, dragging the body to his car, leaving a trail of blood, but taking nothing. The police would later speculate that Mary Hogan had not been the victim of robbery, but perhaps had made an enemy that wanted her gone.

They were only half-right.

***

Ed had a special fascination for the inner organs, cutting out the liver and kidneys and fondling them lovingly. He also liked the female sexual parts, and confessed later to cutting them out and wearing them in a pair of panties. Deep inside himself, Ed wanted to be a woman, wanted to realize the female side of his persona, perhaps as a way to rebel against the stern religious teachings implanted in him by his shrewish, late mother.

It was believed by locals, at this time, that Gein's farmhouse was haunted by the spirit of Augusta, or by some strange female ghost. Locals who drove by the place confessed that they had seen a yellow-skinned nightmare of a woman dancing nude under the moonlight, completing a strange, ritualistic cavort in the yawning, lonely fields. But who could believe such nonsense?

***

Mary Hogan was not the only strange disappearance in the area during this time. Two teenagers, Georgia Weckler and Evelyn Hartly, had both mysteriously gone missing while babysitting. In both cases, there was little evidence for the police to go on except a trail of blood (which suggested foul play in the case of Hartly). Both disappearances would remain unsolved.

***

Ed went into Worden's Hardware store one day wanting antifreeze.

"Hey Eddie, how ya been doing?" asked Bernice, getting Ed what he wanted and carefully ringing up the register.

"Oh, I guess I been okay. Say, Bernice, how about you and I go to the movies together sometime? Fella sure gets lonely going by himself."

Bernice smiled. Ed was such a weird, sweet little man, but he was young enough to be her own son, and she sure wasn't going to give him any encouragement in the strange fixation he seemed to have garnered for her lately.

"Oh Ed, why, I'm old enough to be your mother."

She thought that Ed was probably looking for a mother substitute at any rate. Augusta had been his entire world. She thought it a little sad that Augusta had so warped her child that he was, essentially, a social failure in every regard.

"Well, shucks, Bernice... You can't blame a fellow for trying."

Ed suddenly looked back behind the counter at a stack of hunting rifles for sale. He paused for a moment, then said, "Say, Bernice, I been thinking on getting myself a new gun for this coming hunting season. Mind if I take a look at one of them?"

He nervously fingered the .22 shell in his pocket.

Bernice Worden frowned a little, and went to retrieve a gun for Ed to examine. She thought it an odd request for the spur of the moment, and it made her a little nervous. But it was the middle of the day, and Ed was, after all, strange but harmless.

Ed took the gun and made a show of inspecting it carefully while standing at the counter. Then, while Bernice's attention was diverted, he carefully slipped the .22 shell into the chamber of the rifle, and, with the whisper of the devils that haunted him ringing in his ears, blew Bernice to kingdom come.

He paused for a moment. What was he to do? The report of the rifle had been loud, and now he had the problem of dragging the body away and carting off the evidence to do what he pleased with. He stood there in confusion for a moment. Well, why had he done it anyway?

He left the now familiar trail of blood in his wake, taking the body out back and somehow managing to bundle it into his car. When he was done, he went back in for the cash register; and not because he had any notion of robbery, or to make this murder look like a robbery, but because Eddie Gein was one of those guys that just loved to take things apart and see how they worked.

***

Frank Worden, Bernice's son, was a deputy sheriff.

He was also mighty suspicious of the circumstances surrounding his mother's disappearance. When he heard that crazy Eddie Gein had been spotted going into the hardware store earlier that day, he immediately became distressed.

He found Eddie having supper at the family of some friends in town.

"Eddie, I need to have a word with you," said the Deputy.

Ed stumbled out of the front door onto the rickety porch.

"Well, I can't imagine what about Frank," said Ed, perhaps with a twinkle in his eye.

"Ed, it's Ma. She's disappeared, and I'm afraid something has happened to her."

"Well, if someone is saying I murdered her, then they're just trying to frame me. That's all."

Ed had just given himself away. Deputy Worden took him into custody, and the questioning began.

***

A detachment of deputies was sent out to the Gein place, not knowing exactly what they would find, but each feeling a little nervous anticipation. They each assumed they would find at least the body of Bernice Worden.

They were not prepared for what they would see.

One of them would run from the house, puking, swearing never to set foot back in the place again.

The sheriff made his way back to the station, where he began to pour out a stream of information regarding the horrific discoveries he had made. The officers assembled must have found what he told them hard to believe at first.

Apart from the filth in which Gein existed, there were chairs bolstered with human leg bones, hearts cooking on pans on the stove, a half of a skull used as a food bowl, a box of female vulvas, nine face masks (well-oiled) made from the skin of actual human faces, bedposts adorned with human heads, lips hanging from curtain drawstrings, and on and on.

But, most shocking of all, was the complete female suit, consisting of leggings and torso, that Gein had constructed from the skin of his victims. He confessed that he would don the face masks, torso, and leggings, and go and dance ritualistically under the cover of darkness, hoping to enact a true transformation of himself from his hated male form, to that of the female he secretly always desired to be.

"I feel closer to women when I wear their skin. Especially if they look like my mother."

Ed confessed to killing Mary Hogan, and the horrific aftermath of his murder of Bernice Worden was found in a shed in the back.

Trussed upside down, like a deer, decapitated and eviscerated, her body had been hung by rope from the ceiling. The resultant photographs of this macabre butchery are baffling and sickening, a testament to the proficient degeneracy of a madman and his obsession.

All in all, Ed is believed to have killed two women, and robbed the graves of fifteen others.

Ed was declared mentally unfit to stand trial. His curious smile, his openness concerning his atrocities, and his willingness to take law officers on a tour of his hellish home convinced the judge in the case that he was criminally insane. It would be twelve years before he stood trial for the murders, but the verdict would remain the same.

Charlie Starkweather

Charlie Starkweather one day sat in traffic, his truck running like a great rumbling beast, and cursed everyone in sight. About the incident, he later said:

> The more I looked at people the more I hated them because I knew they wasn't any place for me with the kind of people I knowed. I use to wonder why they was here anyhow. A bunch of goddamned sons of bitches looking for somebody to make fun of, some poor fellow who ain't done nothing' but feed chickens.

Charlie Starkweather was use to being made fun of. Bow-legged, unusually short, uneducated, and with a flaming crop of bright red hair, Starkweather was known as "Little Red" to his friends, and as a sullen, sneaky, no-good sonofabitch to most everyone else. Not that he had many friends.

Charlie had killed his first man when he decided that being a garbage collector wasn't going to pay for the dream life he wanted. It was a cold December day in Lincoln, Nebraska, when he pulled into a Texaco station, his red hair covered with a hat and his face covered in a bandana.

"Give me the damn money, punk!"

Robert Colvert, the station attendant did as he was told, and was then hustled out the back and into Charlie's hot rod. Starkweather drove Colvert out to the plains beyond Lincoln.

Later, police found his frozen body lying in the road.

Two months later, apparently unsatisfied with the measly hundred-dollar take from the heist, Charlie decided it was time to embark, like a rebel hero movie character played by James Dean (who he faintly resembled), on a wild life of crime. He went to visit his fourteen-year-old girlfriend Caril Ann Fugate.

***

Charlie always carried his .22 rifle with him everywhere he went, and this day was no exception.

"Charlie, could you please put that thing away? It's making me nervous!"

Caril Ann's mother, Marion Bartlett, didn't care for Charlie. Or his gun. Charlie sullenly continued to fiddle with the gun, and Mrs. Bartlett started to shout, slapping him across the face.

Charlie hit her back, and when Mr. Bartlett, Caril Ann's stepfather entered the room, the fight was on.

Charlie shot both of them.

By this time, Caril Ann was home from school, and ready to watch her favorite television program. Charlie went into her baby sister's room and thrust the barrel of the gun down the infant's throat until she choked to death. Then the young couple sat in front of the television set together, and cuddled.

***

Charlie carefully covered Mr. Bartlett's body and hid it in the chicken coop, afterwards dumping Mrs. Bartlett into the disused outhouse. Baby Bartlett was unceremoniously deposited in a cardboard box.

Next, he pinned this notice on the door:

> Stay a Way. Every Body is Sick with the Flu.

He figured that would do it. For a little while at least.

***

"Caril Ann! Caril Ann!"

Caril Ann's aunt was at the door. She opened it nervously, bouncing from foot to foot.

"Sorry, but the doctor says not to let anyone in. Everyone here is sick with the flu."

"Caril Ann! You let me in! I need to talk to my sister!"

Caril Ann wouldn't budge, and it was good for her aunt that she wouldn't; Charlie might very well have killed her. Puzzled, the woman went away.

Caril Ann must have known she hadn't heard the last of her aunt, and indeed, several days later, a trio of policemen came calling. They had been alerted by Caril Ann's uncle, who grew suspicious the moment he heard what was going on.

"Well, now," said one of the policemen, "did the doctor say you couldn't let any of your relatives in? I'm sure he didn't say that, did he?"

"Yes he did," protested Caril Ann, "and I wouldn't let anyone in, especially not my Aunt with her baby. Everyone here is sick with the flu."

"Well, Caril Ann, your uncle seemed awful worried about things out here. Why do you suppose that is?"

"I don't know," replied Caril Ann, "but I suppose it is because he never liked me anyway, and is always getting funny ideas in his head."

Unbelievably, the cops bought this for the time being. However, it was not long before Caril Ann's grandmother phoned. Caril Ann was evasive, but warned her grandmother from coming out to the house. The old woman was suspicious, and went to the police herself, finally leading officers (and Starkweather's brother) out to the place.

It had by now dawned on the killer couple that it was unwise to remain around any longer.

They were gone.

Police quickly found the bodies, and the manhunt began. It would encompass the entire Midwest and include 200 National Guardsmen in its ranks.

***

Charlie pulled the car into a service station, mainly to fix a flat, but also to buy ammunition. Caril Ann waited in the passenger seat, like he told her, nervously chewing her nails. Charlie was going to get her into a lot of trouble, she was sure, and she didn't know if she really was up to being along for the ride.

As Little Red sauntered through the aisles of the filling station, the man behind the counter recognized him from the description given over the radio. He debated with himself over going in back and picking up the phone, and it was all he could do to keep from shaking when he handed Charlie back his change. Starkweather, completely unsuspecting, went back out to the parking lot with his purchases, got in his hot rod, and sped away. The counter man rushed to the phone and dialed the police.

***

Inside a lonely farmhouse, a corpse lay sprawled in a Jackson Pollock splatter of brains and grue. Outside, a posse of lawmen had gathered with gas bombs. Sheriff Merle Karnapp had received word that Starkweather's car had been parked outside.

"Come on out, Starkweather! We've got the place surrounded!"

The gas bombs went in the windows, but it was to no avail. Charlie and Caril had already left.

They were, in fact, in the process of committing another crime.

Nearby, in a disused storm cellar, Charlie had two hostages held at gunpoint. Damn fool that he was, he had driven the car into the mud. Well, they had been lucky enough to pick up a ride from two teenagers. And Charlie could see that the girl was quite a looker.

He would make Caril wait outside while he took his pleasure, violently, with her. He made her boyfriend watch. Then he killed them both.

Their names were Robert Jensen and Carol King.

Charlie was pleased. He had a new set of wheels.

He and Caril Ann took off again. Bonnie and Clyde might have been proud.

***

Our duo's next caper took them to the posh residence of one C. Lauer Ward. At first, Charlie wasn't exactly sure of what he wanted there, except that he had never been in a house so glamorous in his life. The place was a veritable mansion. Apparently, the owner had some money.

Charlie pulled up outside, letting the motor idle before casually walking up to the house and asking the maid if he could use the phone. She opened the door to him, smiled, assumed the nice young man and his girlfriend were maybe having car trouble and needed some help.

He walked inside casually, his eyes opening wide as he saw the expensive furnishings, the deep rugs, the swinging crystal chandelier.

"I'll go get the phone," said the maid, leaving him standing in the living room. Suddenly, he could take it no more; the demon welled up inside him, and the bottomless fires of his rage began to burn. He pulled his knife from his pocket, walked up behind the maid, held his hand over her mouth, and said, "Make one peep and that's it, lady!"

Later, he would hustle both the maid and Mrs. Ward upstairs, and tie them up, after ripping their clothes from them violently. That was good. Tied up in their underclothes, gagged, they looked like something from the cover of one of the lurid detective magazines he sometimes liked to flip through. He felt himself grow rigid with delight.

He went out to the car. By now, Caril Ann had wandered up to the house and Charlie invited her in, as if it were their house. She proceeded to help herself to food and whatever goods they could find, and Charlie went into a separate room to consider what his next move should be.

He eventually went back into the upstairs bedroom. His hostages were still firmly bound, writhing in terror on the floor and weeping. He liked that. He enjoyed the power he now wielded over these rich old bitches. His knife was so sharp, he reflected. Why, it would be the work of a moment to make them pay, to cut pieces of their humanity away in a torrent of fury and blood.

And so he stabbed them to death.

He killed one, making the other watch.

Clara Ward and Lillian Fenci were their names.

Caril Ann stayed downstairs while this was going on, but she must have heard the sounds of the killings, heard the muffled screams and the scrambling on the floor and the terrible thuds of the bodies and the sound of the puncturing knife.

Later, Charlie came down to clean up, a bloody mess, and for the first time perhaps, Caril Ann must of realized the full horror of just what her boyfriend had done, and what sort of monster she had decided to take up with.

After ransacking what they could and loading it into their new car (Mr. Ward's 56 Packard) Charlie decided it was probably still too hot for them to take off immediately. He decided to wait there for a few more hours. In that time. Mr. Ward himself would come home from work, never suspecting the horror that awaited him as he stepped through the door.

Charlie promptly blew his head off.

***

By now a police dragnet of considerable size had assembled to lay their hands on Little Red, but somehow the despicable duo managed to make their way into the yawning state of Wyoming. It was here that Charlie would make the mistake of his life.

He would make a Final Stand that would strip him of all dignity in the eyes of the lawmen that finally brought him to justice.

***

Shoe salesman Merle Collison was tired. He had been driving all night, and had decided to pull over and get some shut eye. He was resting peacefully when, all of a sudden, the driver's side window exploded into a million fragments.

"Get out of the damn car!"

Collison moved to comply with Charlie's orders, but he shot him to death anyway. The body slumped across the driver's seat, and the emergency brake became stuck. Charlie yelled over to Caril Ann, saying, "C'mon baby, we got us a new set of wheels!"

Unfortunately for Charlie, the emergency brake refused to yield. When another car came barreling down the road, the driver slowed down, seeing the young man and his little girlfriend at the driver's side door working furiously at the jammed emergency brake.

He pulled over to give them a hand.

He saw the body.

Charlie told him, "Help me with this goddamn break or I'll blow your head off!"

Terrified, the man leaned over to try the break, but managed to grab the rifle from Charlie when his attention was distracted. Suddenly, things were not going well. Charlie yelled and stamped and cursed.

His luck had run out.

A cop car drove by, saw what was going on and screeched to a halt. Caril Ann, finally seeing how things were going to turn out, broke from the trio and ran to the cop car, where she told Deputy Sheriff Rohmer, "Help! It's Starkweather! He's crazy! He's going to kill me!"

Rohmer couldn't get a bead on Starkweather from his position with Caril Ann in the way, so he threw the girl in his squad car, radioing ahead for backup, which, considering how badly wanted Starkweather was (he had made headlines all across the nation) was quick in coming.

Starkweather dove for his car, leading police on a 115 mile an hour chase.

Shots were fired.

Glass exploded.

Starkweather brought the car to a halt, staggering out while holding his bleeding face.

Police Chief Robert Ainsley later smirked, "You're a real tough guy, Charlie."

Charlie had in fact surrendered because he assumed he was shot. He was not. In fact, he only had a minor cut from flying glass.

Starkweather had reached the end of his short, wild ride.

***

The "Rebel Without a Cause" played his role right to the very end.

A picture shows him sprawled out on his prison bunk, his legs spread, curled up at the knees, looking every bit the murderous, two-bit thrill-killing little punk that he was. The expression on his face is insolent, almost amused; Charlie clearly felt no remorse for his sadistically homicidal spree.

The resultant trial was something of a farce.

Charlie had originally thought to play the role of "noble boyfriend," and had insisted that Caril Ann had nothing to do with the murders. Apparently, he thought the law would accept her as merely being a hostage to his whims, and let her go. Caril Ann, perhaps seeing the writing on the wall, even at her young age, immediately turned on Starkweather, protesting, just as he had claimed, that she was too terrified to leave him and that she was essentially along for his spree as a hostage.

This enraged Starkweather, who angrily turned on his former lover in court.

"She could have left anytime she wanted! Why, times when I would go in some place to get hamburgers, she would be sitting in the car with all the guns, waiting. She could have run if she wanted, but she's just as guilty as I am. Once, when she didn't like the food we got, she told me, 'Charlie, we ought to go back to that place and shoot all them people.'"

The jury apparently felt the same way as Charlie. Caril Ann Fugate was sentenced to life in prison. She was finally paroled, in 1976, seventeen years later.

As for her one-time boyfriend, his fate was not so lucky. For his crimes, Charlie Starkweather was sentenced to die in the electric chair, a fate to which he mused, "I'd like to have Caril Ann sitting in my lap when they strap me in."

It was on June 24th, 1959, that Starkweather was led to the death house, after denying a request by the Lions Club that his organs be donated after his execution.

"Hell no!' the James Dean wannabe spat angrily. "Nobody ever done nothing to help me. Why should I do anything to help anybody else?"

He was strapped into the electric chair at Nebraska State Penitentiary and an electric current of 22,000 volts was passed through his body. Half an hour after midnight, he was pronounced dead.

Local reporters saw a disturbing sight, something they took as a sick trend, as they gathered outside the penitentiary to wait word of Starkweather's execution. A group of thirty-odd young men and women, dressed in "Rebel Without a Cause" clothing, and some of them seeming to be nearly in tears. When one young woman was asked why she was there, she replied, "Some of us knowed him. Some of us wanted to be near him at the end."

Police and reporters (and common citizens) must have been chilled by this. Little Red, like many another killer who would come after him, had gained a sort of cult-like notoriety that made of him, however fleetingly, something important, someone to be admired. It was a weird stardom that had been denied Charlie Starkweather during the course of his nineteen bitter, unhappy years.

These might have been the first "death groupies" in history. Like James Dean, Charlie Starkweather, it seemed, had touched a chilling nerve in a discontented, youthful fan base.

Richard Speck

Richard Speck was monumentally ugly, both physically and spiritually. He was a dull man with the mentality of a homicidal dimwit, and no prospects in life besides the restless, unsatisfying existence of a merchant seaman. When he wasn't occupied with work on the docks, he stared dully at comic books. (The comic books, incidentally, he could just barely read.)

No one, least of all Richard, knew how he ended up standing on the steps of the rooming house wherein lived several student nurses. Richard was catastrophically drunk, and believed later that he had injected a substance similar to morphine while at a seedy soiree.

He swayed a little on the front porch, his breath going before him like that of a dragon, and the young woman who answered the door continued to stare at him as if he had just hopped off the latest flight from Mars. No matter. Richard could feel a fire begin to burn within him, and he said, "Hey, can I come in?"

The pretty young Philippine exchange student didn't know how to respond.

Richard pulled out his gun and knife, backing her and three of her friends inside, and slamming the door behind them.

"Don't worry, I'm not going to hurt you. I just need your money. I need to go to New Orleans."

***

Richard had been out of work for some time.

He had drifted into Chicago to seek help from his sister: Her and her husband had given him some money, had driven him to the Maritime Union Hiring Hall that July of 1966, but there was no one hiring. Richard found himself a land-bound sailor, a merchant seaman without a berth. He aimlessly hit skid row bars with buddies of his.

It was on one such excursion that he tried intravenous drugs for the first time. Perhaps it was the influence of these drugs that led, later that day, to the atrocity that Speck would commit, or perhaps it was simply the effects of his own ignorance; ignorance engendered by a steady diet of comic books, trashy media, and little experience with dealing with his own psychological burdens.

His anger over his own terminal unemployment could not have helped. Of course, none of these are even remotely adequate excuses for what Speck was to enact later that evening. That horror would go on to live in infamy in the hearts and minds of a nation shocked at the spectacle of a mass murder perpetrated under the supposedly safe auspices of a shared rooming-house for university nursing students.

The contrast between the monstrous Speck and his innocent victims could not have been more pronounced. America (and we must assume the jury) could look at the beautiful, hopeful faces of the gallery of victims and see a future that was now dimmer for want of the lives of the young girls slain by the bestial loner. Speck, on the other hand, seemed to represent everything that was bad, loathsome, and mindless about American society. Perhaps the monster didn't understand his own inner cravings for sadistic butchery.

***

Speck took the Filipino student, Corazon Amarao, to a back bedroom, where he proceeded to tie her up, as well as six of her fellow nursing students. Tearing strips of cloth from a bed sheet to bind his victims, Speck made sure to keep reminding them that he "didn't intend to hurt them. All I need is the money to make it to New Orleans."

When he finally had them all bound and gagged, he took whatever money he could find and pocketed it. It was at this time that two more of the student nurses returned from a night out. The scene was now set for the horror that Richard Speck was bound to inflict.

We can only imagine what was going on in Speck's mind (such as it was) as he led student nurse Ms. Wilkening to another bedroom, and then threw her down to the floor, stabbing her in the left breast and finishing her off by strangling her with a knotted piece of bed sheet.

***

The stranger had plopped down to the floor and began to play with his gun. He seemed somehow innocent in this moment, child-like in his depravity, and he asked one of the nurses, a Filipino girl that had arrived in United States only a month before, if she knew Karate. The nine girls were terrified, and the stranger seemed to enjoy the sensation of fear he was causing in them.

He selected the pretty one first, getting her up on her feet and into the hall. He took her to another bedroom, hesitated a moment as if unsure of himself, then felt the urgings of the beast give loose inside of him as he stabbed the girl in the left breast.

The man felt his pulse began to quicken, as sexual excitement drove his blood pressure up to the max. The bitch had fallen to the floor and was writhing. That was good. That was exactly what he needed to fulfill his fantasy.

He quickly knotted a length of the torn bed sheet around her throat and began strangling her. He stopped when he could detect no more movement beneath his hands.

He went back into the bedroom where the other girls were bound and gagged. He selected two more, motioning them out and into the hallway. He stopped at the door of another bedroom, and he could feel that primal beast roaring up in him again.

He flashed his knife, fell on one girl, then another. Stabbing and strangling. That was how he was going to complete the night.

He went to the bathroom to wash the blood from his hands. While he was doing so, the terrified girls began to crawl under beds to try and hide from the monster. It seemed to avail them little, however, as Speck had noted the number of his victims as he tied. Even in his delirious, bloodthirsty state, he knew how many he was going to have to kill before there were no more witnesses.

Victim number four was Nina Schmale. Speck ordered her into a bedroom, had her lay down on the bed, and then fell upon her, stabbing her to death. Victims number five and six were the Filipino exchange students Valentina Pasion and Merlita Gargullo, each having only just arrived in the United States a month before.

The monster ordered them out and into another room. He devoured them. They died.

Victim number seven, Patricia Matusek, was taken into the bathroom. There she protested that she wanted to have her bonds loosened. This angered the monster, and he struck out viciously with his foot, kicking her in the stomach and then grabbing her throat. He strangled her to death.

Now, an unexpected thing happened. The monster walked into one of the adjoining bedrooms and found student nurse Miss Davy on one of the beds. Apparently she had been trying to slip away, or, in his mad frenzy of lust and bloodletting, he had somehow managed…to lose count. No matter.

Speck was intensely sexually aroused now, and the sight of Davy on the bed led him to proceed with an act of rape. Corazon Amarao would later describe what she could hear and see from her vantage point beneath the bed as Speck dealt with his final victim.

She said that she could hear the sound of bedsprings, the unzipping of jeans, and other sounds that suggested to her rape. She also heard the monster say, "Could you please put your legs around my back?"

(We can spare the reader the rest.)

Coarazon Amarao waited until she heard no more sounds in the house. Sometime before five that morning, the monster had shambled out of the house after completing his strange, savage work.

At five a.m., the alarm went off as usual. However, none of the silent bodies left in the house would be able to get up and make their rounds at the hospital ever again. All save for Corazon Amarao.

Speck had forgotten one final girl.

He had left a witness.

He had also left behind a policeman's dream of fingerprint evidence.

He was toast. It would only be a matter of time.

However, just then, the Monster didn't realize this at all.

***

He walked the streets feeling like a giant. Sure, the streets of Chicago were mean, but he was meaner. The headlines screamed the news of what he had done. Great. It made him feel special. It made him feel important. It made him feel like Superman and John Wayne and John Dillinger all rolled up into one.

Of course, the Monster knew that he had left one behind. Sure. He had been so excited over it all, had been so turned on and so fuzzy-headed with sheer pleasure, that he had somehow managed to miss this…Amarao. Anyway, he was certain that there was no way that the cops were gonna catch up to him. After all, he now had a certain kind of…power.

He hit the skids. He wanted to drink and raise hell. Hell, he had the words "Born to raise hell" tattooed on him. At last he felt like he deserved a little action. He had finally done something they were gonna remember for a million years.

***

Corazon Amarao had crawled out from her vantage point under the bed, had stumbled over the bodies of her fellow nursing students, and had reeled in disbelief. She apparently was suffering from intense shock, as instead of using the front door, she climbed out of a window onto a ledge and began to scream, partly in her native language of Tagalog.

It was no time before a couple of passersby alerted the police about the woman.

The scene that greeted them inside the townhouse was one of horror and madness.

The police took fingerprints, but they also brought in an excellent sketch artist to give the Monster a face. When they had this impression they published it in the paper.

They also publicized the fact that the only living witness of the massacre was prepared to identify the murderer in court when he was finally apprehended.

This last bit of information did not please the Monster.

***

He let the paper drop to the floor, and climbed atop his bunk.

It was a particularly repellent skid row motel where he was staying, but he had already shot his whole wad of money on hooch and cheap prostitutes, and he was down to his last dollar.

The police were closing in on the Monster, and right now he didn't feel so almighty big anymore. In fact, he felt pretty small, pretty scared. He considered the knife he had in his pocket. He knew there would be one easy way to cure all of his troubles.

Unbeknownst to the Monster the police already had his name, if not his location. A gas station attendant had identified Speck from the police sketch, and told them that the man had recently left bags with him for safekeeping. He also told the police that this man was a merchant seaman that was looking for work.

It took no more than a trip by the police to the Merchant Seaman's Union to ascertain, from a crumpled application to board ship, that the killer they were looking for was one Richard Franklin Speck. The fingerprints lifted from the application were the same as those found at the crime scene. Now they had a name for the Monster, as well as a face.

Ironically, it would be the Monster himself who would ensure that he was brought to justice.

***

The Monster cut into his wrist and arm deeply. It seemed only the fitting and proper thing to do. After all, he had spilled so much of other people's blood recently, why not spill his own in this final act of nihilistic vengeance?

Still, he did not really desire to die. Especially here, in this dollar-a-night flophouse on skid row. He was scared and little, not the big terrifying monster that had committed the horrendous crime that all the tabloids were screaming about. Hell, he was a downright coward when you actually thought about it.

He called out as his blood began to drip onto the mattress.

"Help! Somebody come over here! I done a bad thing!"

The wino in the next room began to scream at him to shut up, so Richard got off his bunk and ambled out into the hallway, trailing his own blood as he went. Somebody standing in the hallway saw what he had done and cried out, "Hey! This guy is trying to bleed himself to death!"

Richard passed out, and was taken to the hospital, where his cuts were attended to. A doctor that had been following the murder investigation in the papers recognized the infamous tattoo "born to raise hell" on Richard's arm, and alerted police. Their first question to the recovering attempted suicide was, "What is your name?"

To which the Monster replied, "Richard. Richard Speck."

Speck was tried and sentenced to death. A media circus ensued around the trial, but finally Speck settled into his role as Death Row inmate and was mostly forgotten. His death sentence was commuted after the Supreme Court overturned the death penalty in 1971, and he was sentenced again to a life term equaling more than four hundred years.

Speck would make national news one other time in his short, sordid life. A video surfaced in the late eighties, apparently shot in prison, of Speck and his homosexual lover sniffing coke, fondling a wad of bills, and having sex. At one point, Speck strips down to a pair of panties and reveals his hormonally-augmented breasts.

The video was splashed across tabloid television, and the public reeled in shock to realize what sorts of activities could take place in a prison under the supposedly watchful eye of authorities.

Speck died in prison of a heart attack in 1991.

Gertrude Baniszewski

One of the most odious criminals in the annals of Indiana history must certainly be the murderous divorcee Gertrude Baniszewski. It is rare that a case can so completely disgust an author that he quite literally finds it impossible to have any sympathetic feelings toward the perpetrator of the crime in question, or to begin to be able to even understand the underlying psychology.

In the case of Baniszewski, however, this is most assuredly the case, as the present author finds her to be, incredibly, the most repugnant character he has yet been taxed to write about.

The story begins in Indianapolis in 1965. Sylvia Likens, and her crippled sister Jenny, were both left in the care for the evening of a rail-thin, asthmatic woman named Gertrude Baniszewski, a woman with six children, including a large, ill-tempered and not-terribly-bright teenage daughter named Paula. Sylvia and Jenny's mother, it seemed, had just been picked up on a minor shoplifting charge. The two young teen girls, both church-goers from a poor home, had a ball spending the night in the rowdy house with their new found friends.

The next day, Mr. Lester Likens bailed his wife out of jail and went looking for his daughters. He had it in mind to get he and his wife a position with a traveling carnival as vendors, a position that would take them to Florida. He felt, almost certainly, that this would be the answer to their financial woes.

He managed to track his daughters down to 3440 New York Street, to a house that was subdivided between two tenants. The Baniszewski clan occupied one side of the ramshackle place, and Mr. Likens was assured by Gertrude that his daughters had been no trouble at all.

Gertrude Baniszewski was a thin, unappetizing woman who was divorced from a local police deputy, John Baniszewski, and who fathered additional children with a much younger man. She was a chain smoker who complained bitterly of asthmatic wheezing and shortness of breath, and who imbibed cough syrup, antihistamines, and "nerve pills" compulsively. She was forever at her lawyer trying to wheedle additional child support out of her ex-husband, and seemed to be just a notch or two above a nervous breakdown, always.

Mr. Likens thanked Mrs. Baniszewski heartily for allowing his daughters to spend the evening with her, and was assured that "one or two extra kids in the house wasn't going to make any difference." Then Mr. Likens did something deeply unfortunate.

He informed Gertrude Baniszewski that he was planning, along with his wife, to take a tour of Florida with a traveling carnival, and suggested that he needed someone to watch his girls while he and his wife were away. Gertrude must have eagerly saw an opportunity to cash in on someone else's misfortunes, for she suggested that Sylvia and Jenny Likens might spend the remainder of the Fall and Summer months with her and her children…for twenty dollars a week. (Which, all things considered, was a not inconsiderable amount of money to buy groceries with in 1965.)

Mr. Likens, not having much in the way of a suspicious nature, immediately assented, and handing over a small amount of money to Gertrude, gathered his daughters and announced to them that they were going to be staying with the Baniszewskis for a little while, while he and mother went out on the road and "patched things up."

The girls were delighted, and in no way could they have foreseen what was to occur later, as the days and weeks rolled forward.

At first, everything seemed fine, if a little strained. Gertrude did not work, save to take in laundry and washing, and the girls were sent to school along with the other children. The honeymoon was not to last long, however.

Food became scarce in the large, ill-kempt household, and Sylvia and her sister were fed almost nothing after a week, save for bread and margarine, and soup in the evenings. In the end, this would go down to a diet of saltine crackers, and both of the girls would literally find themselves starving. (Gertrude's children, we must assume, were given much more.)

Still the young girls did not complain, and Sylvia was happy to have the food offered her at school and an occasional church supper. Of course, when Gertrude found out that Sylvia and Jenny were getting extra food, it brought out the steadily mounting psychotic rage inside of her, and she began the series of strange and sadistic "disciplines" that would, finally, result in tragedy.

Sylvia was beaten with a large, fraternity-style wooden paddle, as was Jenny, both punishments meted out for the crime of daring to have more to eat than Gertrude's own malnourished brood. This was terrible enough, but it was only the beginning.

Gertrude's daughter Paula, a large, frumpy, painfully unattractive eighteen-year-old, became convinced that Sylvia (who all accounts state was a well-behaved, quiet, and helpful child) was spreading rumors among friends at school about her being pregnant. When Paula told her mother this, Gertrude became predictably unhinged, and prescribed as a punishment for Sylvia that she strip naked and perform lewd acts with a coke bottle in front of her children and other youngsters from the neighborhood.

Then she began to burn Sylvia with cigarettes.

This would become habitual for Gertrude.

One of the great mysteries of the case has always been the reaction both of the Baniszewski children and the neighborhood playmates, and the casual way they meted out brutality to Sylvia, just accepting the daily abuse as if it were all part of some normal childhood game. Of course, they were encouraged by the only adult in the household, Gertrude, who as the weeks progressed, began to descend more and more into actual sadistic torture when it came time to meet out "punishment" to her favorite punching bag, Sylvia Likens.

Both Johnny Baniszewski and his oafish, criminal friend Coy Hubbard were encouraged to try out their judo moves on Sylvia, and Coy became renowned for flipping the young girl over his shoulder and sending her to the wooden floor with a crash. Neighborhood children were encouraged to come over and "play" with Sylvia by punching, kicking, pulling her hair, and putting matches out on her skin; and, of course, the chain-smoking Gertrude also found ample opportunity to extinguish her smokes on Sylvia's skin. The situation, the reader will note, went from being bad to nearly surreal very quickly.

Ricky Hobbs, a fourteen-year-old boy who, it has been suggested, Gertrude let hang around with the intention of eventually seducing, was likewise encouraged to burn, beat, and abuse Sylvia, but did so less frequently, perhaps realizing intuitively that, eventually, they would all be called to answer for the crimes of abuse they were committing.

Ricky, though, would play an important role in what was to become one of the defining characteristics of the crime.

By this time, Sylvia had dropped school completely, perhaps embarrassed at having to parade around black and blue, and was confined to the living hell of the Baniszewski home where she was eventually thrown (literally) down the basement stairs and made to sleep on a filthy mattress below. She would be thrown down the rickety basement stairs several times before it was all over.

Paula Baniszewski proved as equally sadistic as her mother, and was given to beating Sylvia with whatever object came handy: bottles, a lamp, curtain rods, etc. She once boasted at church that she broke her wrist on Sylvia's jaw, "To teach her a lesson!" The church youth group leader apparently had no reply to this, thought it none of his business, and, like all the neighbors who *must* have heard the screams and the beatings, decided to ignore something they "didn't want to get involved in." Paula occasionally beat Sylvia with her cast.

But this is still not the worst.

The last week or two of her life were, predictably, the worst for Sylvia. She had been beaten and starved to a point of physical shock, and Gertrude (who in her addled mind was now convinced that Sylvia was the worst whore in the world) had at one point tied her to an upstairs bed, refused to let her go to the restroom, denied her any food or water, thrown her back down in the basement, forced her to eat feces and drink urine, beat her across the head with a paddle, and then enlisted the help of the children to bind Sylvia hand and foot and give her a series of scalding hot baths to "cleanse the sin of her whoredom."

She was again deposited in the basement. When Ricky Hobbs came over that weekend, he found Gertrude attempting to carve words in Sylvia's chest with a searing hot needle.

Ricky, always a helpful boy, obliged to do the honors. They carved a bloody tattoo across Sylvia's emaciated chest. It read:

I'M A PROSTITUTE AND PROUD OF IT

Sylvia was held down by the other children, as this was done in full sight of them. Of course, to the cruel little children it must have seemed like some sort of bizarre game. After all, Gertrude was the adult, and she was the one who had instigated it.

Curiously, the children were then encouraged to heat up a pair of metal scraps in the form of an "S" to brand Sylvia with. They failed at this, holding the pieces the wrong way, and so Sylvia's body was branded with an ubiquitous "3" instead. Jenny Likens knew that time was running out for her sister, but, foolishly, she still believed that Gertrude would eventually relent and get Sylvia medical attention.

Gertrude had other things in mind though. She had not long before suggested taking Sylvia out to the woods and "dumping" her. To this end, she forced Sylvia to compose a letter to her parents, a bizarre document outlining a series of juvenile indiscretions and weaving a tale of Sylvia being waylaid by a gang of rapists… Gertrude already must have known that her sadistic games were going to get her in a lot of trouble, and that it would be better for her if Sylvia suddenly "disappeared," as if abducted by sexual predators.

In other words, Gertrude was already stewing over how she was going to outright murder the girl and get rid of her body.

Sylvia Likens' last weekend of life was a cruel, punishing experience. She was forced to masturbate with a Pepsi bottle, tied up in the basement by Johnny Baniszewski torture-rack style, and, when it became apparent that the girl was quickly succumbing to the brutal treatment, she was forced upstairs where Gertrude tried to force her to eat some donuts. When Sylvia failed to comply, Gertrude smashed her in the stomach. Later, she beat her with curtain rods until the rods bent at right angles, and Coy Hubbard threw her back downstairs into the basement.

Gertrude must have had a dawning realization that Sylvia had been abused beyond the point of no return, as it was at this time that she forced Sylvia to write the phony letter saying she had been raped by a gang of boys. Later, the police would be unconvinced by this scrawled confessional.

Stephanie Baniszewski came home from school and found Sylvia too sick to move. The girl was clearly having trouble breathing (she had in fact told her sister Jenny shortly before, "Jenny, I know you don't want me to die, but I'm going to die. I can tell."), and her chewed lips and swollen throat were unable to take any food.

Stephanie and Johnny Baniszewski carried Sylvia to an upstairs back bedroom and laid her down on a mattress. The girl was delirious, and said, "I want my Daddy." She implored Stephanie Baniszewski (who had been less involved in the abuse than any of the other children) to "take her home."

She also said that "all her teeth felt loose."

Gertrude was stumbling through the halls in a hysterical frenzy of fear, crying, "She's faking! She's faking!" She stopped in the doorway of the room where Sylvia was dying and started to scream before Stephanie, in a fit of rage, told her mother to shut up and get out. She tried to perform mouth to mouth. She demanded that Johnny Baniszewski call the police, and he did. It was too late, however.

Sylvia Likens was dead.

The photos of her branded corpse, with the ubiquitous "3" and the words "I'M A PROSTITUE AND PROUD OF IT" horrified any who saw them, and the marks of abuse from beating, starvation, and cigarette burns (the autopsy revealed more than one hundred scars from cigarette burns) were apparent. The death of Sylvia Likens sent shock waves across the nation. Something had gone wrong in America, when a teenage girl could be beaten and starved to death in a placid American neighborhood, while no one stepped in to do anything to stop it.

Gertrude, predictably, tried to lay the blame at the feet of her children and their friends. Her daughter Paula, Richard Hobbs, Coy Hubbard, and Johnny Baniszewski were all indicted for first-degree murder. The rest of the Baniszewski children were given over to foster homes.

The trial revealed the full and awful extent of the "mob mentality" as it applied to a group of impressionable children. The children themselves couldn't, for the life of them, figure out what had made them each be so cruel to Sylvia Likens, except that "everyone else was doing it," and the adult in the house, Gertrude Baniszewski, had sanctioned it. Under cross-examination, Gertrude Baniszewski became belligerent, complained of not being able to breathe, claimed that it was the children who were responsible for the brunt of the torture and abuse, and claimed that she was in bed ill most of the time with asthma and mental problems. The jury wasn't buying it, not after seeing the death photos of Sylvia Likens.

Her insanity plea failed miserably, and even her own lawyer, in closing argument, suggested that he thought she should go to the electric chair (a prospect that sent Gertrude visibly reeling in the courtroom). In the end, she was convicted of first-degree murder, and sentenced to life imprisonment. Her codefendants, being minors, were sentenced to a youth reformatory. They would each be released within a few years.

Paula Baniszewski served a few years, as did Johnny Baniszewski, Ricky Hobbs, and Coy Hubbard. Hubbard would go on to become an habitual criminal, and would serve several prison terms. Ricky Hobbs would die of cancer at twenty-one, and Johnny Baniszewski would go on to change his name and become a preacher in Texas. He later admitted in an interview that he felt that the punishment he received for his part in the murder wasn't nearly hard enough.

Gertrude received life, narrowly escaping the electric chair, and served twenty years. Reportedly, when asked the motive for what she had done to Sylvia Likens, the only rationalization she could make was "to teach her a lesson," whatever that meant.

Gertrude served twenty years and was paroled in 1985. She died five years later in Iowa, of lung cancer. It is the opinion of this author that Gertrude Baniszewski got off far, far too easy for what she did to Sylvia Likens.

And the author is usually not a very vindictive person.

John Wayne Gacy

John Wayne Gacy, whatever else might have been true of him, was never going to look or behave like his famous Hollywood namesake. That was one fact of his life that was undeniable.

His father was a big, violent tempered Polish immigrant who beat the family ceaselessly and drank himself to an early grave. John admired and loathed him in equal measure. When the old man died, John blamed his own conviction for a sexual assault as being the cause. It wasn't, but the fact that John thought it was gives a telling example of his mental state.

John Wayne Gacy was born in 1942, the son of a machinist who wanted him to be a real mensch, a "tough guy." As John Jr. grew up, it immediately became apparent that he was never going to be able to live up to his father's expectations.

For one thing, he had a congenital heart defect that kept him from playing many of the rough-and-tumble games that delighted the other boys in the neighborhood. This embarrassed his father enough. But when the boy, who had always seemed to have oddly feminine ways and interests, began to take up after his sisters, to share their interest in girly things like dolls and quilting, the elder Gacy realized his young son had a desperate problem. At least in his opinion.

By all accounts, the elder Gacy was a vicious tyrant that drank himself crazy all afternoon, and would then come to the table and sit down with a family that was hushed in fear and terror of his frequent rages.

It is reported that the elder Gacy beat his children with a wire strap, but that John refused to cry during these beatings. If so, we can surmise that he was saving up a huge well of rage and terror that would explode later in the holocaust that he was to create.

***

As a young man, John Wayne Gacy suffered a severe head trauma when he was hit in the head with a swing. Whatever effect this might have had on the mind of the budding killer can only be a matter of speculation, but it has been assumed by some that this was the genesis of his homicidal obsession. Whatever the case, Gacy grew up in the shadow of his abusive father, went on to business school, and after graduation, moved to Iowa, where he married and bought into the franchise of a fast food restaurant.

All was not to remain well in Gacy's world, however, as the slumbering beast of his depraved sexual urges soon got the better of him. He lured one of his underage employees into the back, and propositioned the young man for sexual favors. Gacy was quickly rebuffed, so he simply attacked the boy and tried to force him into homosexual acts.

The young man broke away from Gacy's grip, and when he told his parents, the police quickly stepped into the situation.

Of course, Gacy denied everything, and even went so far as to hire some local hoodlums to try and terrify the boy into not testifying. This backfired on him miserably, as the boy was outraged enough to boldly go before the court. Gacy was convicted of child molestation and given a ten year sentence.

He was released after only eighteen months.

He could find nothing for him in Iowa, and his wife had already decided she wanted nothing else to do with him, so he packed up and went back to Chicago in 1971. Here, Gacy planned to remake himself, to transform himself from the socially repugnant ex-con child molester into someone who would truly be respected and admired to all who know him. Or, at the very least, knew him by his exterior mask of sanity.

Gacy went to work in construction, and was soon operating a contracting firm that was bringing the money rolling in. He joined the Junior Chamber of Commerce, was a respected member of the Jaycees, and married again. He bought a ranch-style home at 8213 West Summerdale in Des Plaines, an address that would later become infamous.

When not hobnobbing in Democratic Party circles or having his picture taken with Rosalynn Carter, Gacy showed the "warm and fuzzy" side of his putrid personality by entertaining at children's hospitals, dressed as "Pogo the Clown," a carnival character of his own creation.

Some have noted that Gacy's makeup as "Pogo" was anything but cheery and lighthearted, and was really rather skull-like; they guess his intention in creating this particular character was actually to frighten, rather than amuse, sick children.

Whatever the case, the hideous clown would become a sort of Gacy trademark. He would even become known, popularly, as the "Killer Clown."

Wedded bliss was not to be John Gacy's lot in life. His wife soon decided that her closeted homosexual husband, who, likewise, had the added disadvantage of possessing a violent, sadistic temper, was rather not to her liking, and left him forthwith. John Gacy may have found this troubling, as it blew a hole in the carefully cultivated image he had tried so hard to build since his release from prison, but it did not stop him from doing what he liked to do: namely, cruising homosexual gathering spots like "Bughouse Square" in Chicago, looking for young boys.

Some of the trepidation Gacy's second wife had about him may have been caused by a little legal run-in over a young male he had picked up the year he came to Chicago. Gacy had tried to force the young man to have sex with him, but was understandably rebuffed (Gacy was, even then, corpulent and seedy). Later the boy refused to testify against him and the charges were thrown out.

Gacy was cruising gay areas for young hustlers heavily by 1977, usually using the pretext of bringing them over to his house to discuss hiring them for a "job," with the only real job Gacy having in mind being the satisfaction of his sick, demented pleasure.

By 1978, Gacy was killing his young victims regularly, disposing of their bodies by burying them in the increasingly crowded confines of his crawlspace.

***

The boy stood on the corner, smoking a cigarette. Suddenly, a car pulled up to him. Behind the wheel, a heavy man with sweat dotting his forehead.

It was a nice car. Real nice.

"Hey. Hey guy. You want to take a ride with me? I got a job for you."

"Sure you have. Pervert."

The man leaned out of the window. He had three chins, bags under his eyes, and was sweating profusely, even though it wasn't hot.

"Hey, man, don't be like that. That's not what I meant. Nothing like that. I just want to know if you're looking for a job. Hey, I'm in construction. I'm always looking for young guys to help out. You look pretty strong to me. You interested?"

The young man threw his cigarette away, looked at the guy in the car, and realized this was probably just a come-on by some fat pervert. But what if it wasn't? What if the guy was legit? Maybe he really did have a construction company. Hell, he had a nice enough car.

The young man got in. It was to be the worst mistake of his entire life.

Gacy was charming during the drive, a big, likable fellow who obviously got a kick from just helping people out. When they got to the house, John even offered to show the young man a few of the magic tricks that he used to entertain children when he was dressed as Pogo the Clown.

One of them was a handcuff escape.

The boy found that he couldn't get free from the handcuffs, though.

John waved the key in front of his face.

He quickly slipped a rag filled with chloroform over the boy's face.

"Lights out," he laughed.

***

The boy woke up with his hands and feet bound. Gacy was standing naked before him, his fat, hairy body jiggling repulsively with glee. Gacy began holding up various whips and sex toys.

"You're so beautiful. So beautiful. But…you're worthless scum! I'd kill you just as soon as look at you."

The boy felt his drugged head bob. He could barely believe what he was seeing.

Gacy began to use his whips and torture devices. The young man screamed. Gacy decided that he was making too much noise, bringing the chloroform rag up to the young man's mouth and nose again. The boy passed out. Woke up. Was tortured. Passed out again…on and on into the night. He was in so much pain at one point that he begged Gacy to kill him.

Amazingly, Gacy did not kill the boy.

Instead, he dumped his unconscious body off in Lincoln Park, at the base of a statue. John was sure that the kid wouldn't cause him any trouble, or he almost assuredly would have killed him.

(Perhaps Gacy was becoming worried that the crawlspace beneath his house was becoming overstocked?)

The boy went to the hospital. The sexual assault had badly injured him, and he was told by the doctors that the chloroform had permanently injured his liver.

The police told him there was little they could do without the man's identification, and the boy became enraged. He vowed to hunt down his assailant himself.

The only memory marker he had to go by, however, was an exit ramp. So there he parked, day after day, waiting for the black Oldsmobile to come roaring by.

When it finally did, he followed it for a short while, and made sure to get the license number. The boy could feel himself closing in, the prey having now become the predator.

When the license plate was checked against county records, it proved that the car belonged to one John Wayne Gacy.

However, even though the boy was now able to obtain an arrest warrant against Gacy, because of a technicality due to jurisdiction, police claimed they were unable to complete it. The boy continued to pressure them, realizing that every day that John Gacy was a free man put other young men such as himself at risk.

Finally, a warrant was issued against Gacy for a misdemeanor battery. Gacy shrugged off his newest arrest, and offered to pay six thousand dollars of medical expenses to his victim. Why the police did not choose to charge Gacy with a felony at this time remains unclear.

On December 11th, 1978, the mother of a young boy named Robert Piest went into the Des Plaines Illinois police station to report that her son had "gone off with a contractor to discuss a possible job…and was now missing." It only took a talk with the pharmacist at the drug store in which the young man was last seen to ascertain that this "contractor" was Gacy.

At that point, Gacy was called, but denied having any knowledge of the Piest boy, or having even met with him. While he was denying this he was actively making plans to smuggle the Piest boy's body out of the house and throw it in the river, as he had three others.

***

Detective Kozenczak was certain that he had his man. But the fat bastard was playing hard, and he insisted he had to make an "important" phone call just then. He was stalling, Kozenczak knew, but the detective was nothing if not patient.

"It's okay. We'll wait."

Gacy took forever on the phone. This was deliberate, of course. When he finally slammed the phone down, he said, "Look, I have a lot of important work to do around here! I don't have time to go down to the station to answer any questions! I don't care about some missing kid! It means nothing to me."

Detective Kozenczak said, "Well, it means a lot to the parents…" but he wasn't ready for Gacy's belligerence. He politely dropped off a card and asked that Gacy drop by the station when he had the time. He then went to a judge and got an immediate search warrant.

The warrant was served on Gacy, and a receipt made out to Piest from the pharmacy cinched the fact that Gacy and Piest had had contact. Still, it was not enough detectives felt.

They put a tail on Gacy, having him watched at all hours. Gacy knew he was under surveillance, and made the best of it from his viewpoint: toying with his police escort by driving around at all hours and under breakneck conditions. Gacy was coming apart at the seams, and the detectives knew it would be just a matter of time before he cracked.

It was December 19th, 1978, when Gacy finally did crack, committing one of the most bizarre acts of his monstrous life. He peered out the venetian blinds of his living room and saw the two detectives sitting out in their car, watching his house. He decided, suddenly, to go out and greet them.

"Hiya fellows. Say, it's kinda chilly out here. You guys want to come in and get a cup of coffee?"

The detectives must have looked at each other in amazement for a moment, but it didn't take long before one of them said, "Sure John. That sounds like it would be great."

They followed Gacy into his sprawling house. Right away one of them noticed a peculiar, strong odor. Where had he smelled that odor before?

"Oh, never mind the smell," explained Gacy. "I'm having trouble with a valve on my sump pump. Makes the whole place smell kind of funny, doesn't it?"

John busily made the coffee while the detectives ambled around, trying to figure out where the smell was coming from, and where they had smelled it before. Suddenly, one of them knew.

It was the same smell as he smelt when he entered the city morgue.

It was the smell of decaying bodies.

For Gacy, the jig was up.

***

Twenty-nine bodies, in various states of decomposition, were found buried beneath Gacy's house. His miraculous and comic explanation for this was that he had several keys loaned out to his house, and that the bodies must have been killed and placed there by other people. Predictably, the jury failed to be convinced by this argument.

This did not deter Gacy from elaborating on this ridiculous defense for the next fourteen years.

While he was on death row, Gacy's notoriety increased because of his steady stream of paintings, most rendered in a bizarre, amateurish "paint by numbers" fashion, or subjects ranging from his beloved Pogo the Clown, to dwarves, rock stars, fellow serial killers, skulls, Hitler, macabre scenes, etc. These became quite popular and were at one point, selling for thousands of dollars. Like wise, Gacy wrote to and befriended many admirers, including notorious punk rock musicians like G.G. Allin and The Cramps, several of which used Gacy artwork for album covers.

He also began a pen pal relationship with eighteen-year-old Jason Moss, a young man whose fascination with serial killers led him to contact several of them. Recounted in his book, *The Last Victim*, Moss found that while Gacy could be superficially charming, he was still obsessed with sexual control, violence, and psychological manipulation. One letter sent by Gacy to Moss states:

> ...I did not kill or murder anyone, I owned the property so they want you to assume I did. They say I confessed, but have no confession when asked in court. I have had three hours of truth serum, showing that I had no knowledge of some 28 victims, and the five I knew about, it wasn't about killing them. That's not admissible in court. I was sold out by my own attorneys for book rights. That's what I've have been appealing all of these years. But I am an embarrassment on the criminal justice system, because if I am right then they are wrong, and too many careers and money have been made off my name, and for political reasons its better to kill me than to let the public know they f#$%#& up fifteen years ago.

However, the bulk of Gacy's correspondence, according to Jason Moss, revolved around Gacy's attempted seduction of himself, and efforts to get Jason to seduce his own brother.

As if this wasn't bad enough, Jason went to visit Gacy on death row a few months before his scheduled execution. At first thinking that his visit with Gacy would be safe and monitored, Jason soon found out that Gacy had arranged things so as to enable Jason to give him expected sexual favors while he was at the prison. At one point, Gacy exposed himself, began fondling himself, and commanded Jason to service him, while exhorting that he could "stab a pen" into Jason's neck, and that he would be dead before the guards could ever get there to stop him.

Although nothing occurred, Jason Moss had had enough of this sort of treatment, and did not return to visit Gacy again. He later went on to write his bestselling book, as well as intern for the Secret Service.

John Wayne Gacy was executed by lethal injection May 10, 1992.

Alton Coleman

The notion that serial killers are all deranged white males is a common misperception. Women, as well as minorities, are included in the ranks of serial killers, although white males do make up the largest percentage.

Such is the case of Alton Coleman, a black man who went through several Midwestern states, killing other African Americans indiscriminately, preying mainly on children.

Coleman had previously been in prison for the crime of child molestation, and upon his release began a series of crimes so atrocious as to bugger belief.

Often treated to the sight of his mother servicing her clients in front of him, Alton Coleman grew up the son of a prostitute, as did his fellow serial killer Henry Lee Lucas. His maternal grandmother raised Coleman, his living situation with his mother having become intolerable. By a young age, he had already garnered a warped view of the world, and this could not have been helped by the fact that childhood bullies referred to little Alton Coleman as "Pissy," a nickname he acquired because of his inability to stop urinating himself.

"Pissy" Coleman grew into young adulthood with a festering hatred of women and an inability to control his more animalistic urges. He was already well known to the police due to a number of early sex-offences, and, indeed, by the time he started his deadly spree was under indictment for the rape and murder of a fourteen-year-old girl. Coleman, not seeing his case as very promising, decided it would be in his best interest to take off.

He hit the bloody road, leaving Wisconsin for Gary, Indiana.

Somewhere long the line he met up with Debra Brown. Brown was described as being mildly mentally retarded, and furthermore was engaged to be married to another man when she first met Coleman. Coleman, who, as many serial killers can attest to, was able to lay the charm on thick when he wanted to, swept Brown off her feet and into the world of serial murder.

Unbeknownst to her, her new paramour was hiding some rather bizarre personal habits right from the start. He was a man who, apparently, was well known to law enforcement as the type of individual that would engage in sexual relations at any time, anywhere, with anyone, under any circumstances. He was also said to enjoy dressing in women's clothing (Note: this should not be construed as a slur against transvestites, who are typically passive, peaceful people. We mention it only as a fact of the case.), and he had beaten the rap on four different sexual assault cases in the past, often by intimidating witnesses, conning the courts, and just plain sheer dumb luck. What he called his "voodoo."

He had spent time in prison on sexual assault charges as well as robbery, but these were all short stretches. As a child, he enjoyed breaking windows and setting things on fire. Such were the ways of Alton Coleman. He was no boy scout.

His first murders were of two young girls, Annie and Tamika Turks. Coleman and Brown abducted both, and Annie was forced to watch while Brown held Tamika down, Coleman then proceeding to jump on her chest with his full weight. Both Coleman and Brown then sexually assaulted Annie, who was then beaten about the head until she was very near death.

Miraculously, she survived, although the horrifying ordeal left her physically and emotionally scarred for life.

Brown and Coleman dumped Tamika's body, and went right to work again on their next victim.

They committed a home invasion in Dearborn Heights, at the residence of Palmer Jones and his wife. They handcuffed and beat Mr. and Mrs. Jones before stealing their money, and then their car. This they later dumped, as they had others.

Donna Williams, 25, of Gary was reported missing. On July 11th, her decomposed corpse was found in Detroit. So was her car. So was a forged ID with Debra Brown's picture on it. Law enforcement was now just about certain who they were looking for.

Apparently, for some reason the duo had decided to dump the car. The body they had dumped right after they finished strangling the life out of it.

July 5th, 1984. Alton Coleman and Debra Brown blew into Toledo Ohio, where they immediately befriend a young woman named Virginia Temple, a woman with several young children. Relatives of Virginia Temple become concerned when she is not heard from for several days. They quickly go to the home...and find frightened children milling about. However, where are Virginia and her oldest daughter, Rachelle?

Simple. They are in the crawlspace, where Coleman and Brown left them after robbing and killing them.

Coleman and Brown had already committed another serious home invasion just that morning, entering the home of the Duvendack's and beating and binding them before robbing them blind. They had then stolen the car. The Duvendack's, however, got off comparatively light.

They befriended a local pastor and by July 9th, felt comfortable enough with him to attend religious services, and get a ride from him to Cincinnati, where Coleman might have felt the trail was a little less hot. By now, the FBI had added Coleman as a special addition to its list of Ten Most Wanted fugitives.

It was in Cincinnati that Coleman suffocated to death fifteen-year-old Tonnie Storey. Later, Coleman and Brown approached the home of Harry Walters, a man who had a camper for sale in his front yard. Coleman presented himself very cordially, but Mr. Walters must have known that something was amiss.

The stranger did not look like he had any money to buy anything, let alone a camper. And there was something about the way Coleman kept fidgeting around in his seat, and then would get up to pace the floor of the living room, that must have raised red flags in the old man's mind.

Red flags or not, however, it was a lightening fast piece of work that Coleman did as he grabbed the heaviest object he could find and brought it down on Mr. Walters' head, repeatedly. He beat the old man to the floor, while Debra subdued the wife, who had come in from another room shouting.

That was bad, thought Alton Coleman. The old bitch had shouted, and could have possibly alerted someone close by to what they were doing in here. She would have to pay, he decided.

Coleman and Brown beat Mrs. Walters to death.

When their daughter, Sheri, made it home from work at half past three, she was treated to a gruesome discovery. Both of her parents were lying at the bottom of the basement steps. They had both been bound with electrical cord, and both had been beaten severely. Her mother was already cold. The coroner later found that bits of Mrs. Walters' brain and skull were missing.

The house looked like it had been the scene of a massacre. Blood was on the walls, stairs, and floor, and bloody footprints and a broken soda bottle bore Coleman's fingerprints. The car, a red Plymouth, was predictably gone, along with an amount of cash and jewelry.

It was in Evanston, Illinois that the couple was apprehended, oddly enough. It was a coincidence: A former acquaintance recognized Coleman from the old neighborhood in Milwaukee as Coleman and Brown were crossing the street to go into a park. The acquaintance quickly drove to a gas station and alerted the police.

There they found the deadly duo sitting on some bleachers. Brown tried to leave the park as she saw the police approach. They found a gun in her purse.

Coleman at first tried to deny that he was, indeed, *that* Alton Coleman, the one that was wanted by the FBI. But the police quickly identified him, and the demented duo's crime spree was now at an end.

Police quickly found themselves with a predicament. Coleman had committed numerous murders in several different states. Which one would be the best to try him in?

For instance, in Wisconsin he had killed Vermita Wheat.

He had killed in Gary, Indiana.

In Detroit Michigan.

In Cincinnati, Ohio, and in Illinois.

He had also killed in Kentucky.

(Getting the play-by-play details of the Coleman crime spree can be a confusing undertaking. We hope we have conveyed as much as needed to underscore the brutality of this singular, "disorganized" serial killer. We have yet to come across an authoritative body count for Coleman.)

It was finally decided that Ohio would be the best, most likely place for Coleman to receive the death penalty. And sure enough, in 1985, both Brown and Coleman were extradited to Ohio, where they were quickly convicted of the murders of Storey and Walters, and given death sentences.

But it didn't end there.

He was likewise given a death sentence in Indiana for the killing of Tamika Turks, and then again in Illinois, where he acted as his own attorney, apparently forgetting the old adage that: "Any man who acts as his own attorney has a fool for a client."

He received yet another death sentence, making him the only man in history to have four death sentences in the U.S. at the same time. He took his case to the Supreme Court several times, arguing that he had insufficient counsel, a brain dysfunction, and that his execution was, hence, unconstitutional. He also argued, almost comically, that since there were so many survivors and family members wishing to be witnesses to his execution, that it would turn his date with the reaper into, in effect, a "spectator sport."

All of this was to no avail. His last meal was a sumptuous feast of steak smothered in onions, fried chicken breasts, broccoli and cheese, salad, sweet potato pie, collard greens, cornbread, French fries, onion rings, and biscuits and gravy. For his beverage he enjoyed a cherry cola.

He went to his death April 26th, 2002. Debra Brown is currently incarcerated in Ohio, having had her sentence commuted, although she is reportedly completely unrepentant.

As was Alton Coleman.

Laurie Dann

Laurie Dann was a curious girl.

Friends recall her riding elevators up and down for hours, leaving raw meat in sofa cushions, and using a pair of rubber gloves to touch common items in her filthy apartment in Evanston, Illinois.

She would flick television channels back and forth for hours, had an obsession with numbers, and was moved briefly to Wisconsin to be put under the supervision of a psychiatrist, one who specialized in OCD (Obsessive Compulsive Disorder). Her family begged her to be admitted as an inpatient on a psychiatric unit, but she steadfastly refused, possibly due to paranoia. She was prescribed drugs like lithium and clomipramine, but these seemed to do little to alleviate her psychiatric problems.

Laurie purchased a gun, a .22 semi-automatic Berreta, and seemed to be making some nefarious plans. She read books on poisons, shoplifted wigs and garments from various stores, and was even apprehended for this at one point. Curiouser and curiouser.

In 1988, a janitor had found Laurie Dann lying in a garbage sack in a trash room, unconscious.

She sent threatening letters to in-laws, and generally raised as many red flags as a psychopath can before they enact whatever it is they seem to be stewing over internally.

But what was Laurie Dann's secret plan?

***

Dann accused her old psychiatrist of trying to rape her. She accused her husband of raping her with a steak knife. She made dozens of threatening phone calls to a former boyfriend and in-laws, and, since these calls crossed state lines, Laurie was the subject of a pending federal indictment.

Laurie Dann stole some diluted arsenic while she lived in Madison, Wisconsin. She took this concoction back with her to Evanston, Illinois. There, she made juice cups and snack treats for a whole slew of her perceived enemies: in-laws, her former psychiatrist, former babysitting clients, etc.

(Did we mention Laurie made her money chiefly from babysitting?)

She delivered some of these poisoned snacks herself, and sent others through the mail. It was May 20th, 1988, and Laurie Dann, crazier than a shithouse rat, was due for her date with destiny.

Dann's activities for the day boggle the mind.

She started off by picking up two young boys she often babysat for, promising to take them on a little outing. She took them on an outing alright: straight to the Ravinia Elementary school, where she attempted to explode an incendiary device in the hallway. Dann's choice of that particular school might have been influenced by the fact that two of the children of a former in-law were enrolled there.

Failing this mission (the fire was extinguished by a teacher); Dann fled the scene with her two young passengers, coming next to a daycare where another in-law had a child enrolled. Here she tried to enter with a gasoline can, but was rebuffed at the door, we think wisely.

Dann then drove back to the home of the two boys, gave them some cool, refreshing drinks of poisoned juice (which they spat out due to the taste) and got the whole family trapped in the basement before setting fire to the house. The family, thankfully, narrowly escaped.

Dann was then off, armed with three handguns, and drove to the Hubbard Woods Elementary School, where she observed a second grade classroom working, before going into the washroom, pushing a young boy inside and shooting him with the twenty-two, then pulling her 357. Fortunately, it jammed, and two young boys went screeching out of the washroom.

Dann then reentered the classroom she had been in previously, struggled with the teacher (who managed to unload one of the guns) shot at several groups of cowering students with the other, and then fled.

She managed to kill eight-year-old Nicholas Corwin and wounded four others.

Bloody but undaunted, Dann found the roads impassable, so abandoned her car and stripped off her jeans, tying a garbage sack around her waist. She then struck out for the woods.

***

"Help! Help! Oh my God, I've just shot a man!"

Laurie stumbled, half-naked, into the Andrew residence. Mrs. Andrew and her son, Phillip, were in the kitchen. At seeing the woman enter their house in such a state, waving a gun, they both felt their jaws drop open. Both were speechless.

"Help me, help me, oh God! Some man tried to rape me! I–I shot this man! Oh God! It was self-defense, I swear it. I swear it!"

Phillip Andrew got up from the kitchen table slowly and approached the young woman with his hands outstretched. He tried to remain as calm and cool as he possibly could, under the circumstances.

"Okay, it's going to be okay Miss. Now, just give me the gun--"

"No!"

"Look, just give me the gun, and we'll call the police and see what we can do about this. I'm sure they'll understand what happened if you were raped..."

Suddenly, Phillip's mother said, "I have an old pair of jeans you can put on. Here let me go get them, and you can take that thing off, okay."

Laurie seemed a little relieved at this, and followed Mrs. Andrew into the back bedroom to get the jeans. While she went, she set down her 22. Gun and Phillip quickly pocketed this. His mind was racing. He didn't know, just then, that Laurie Dann still had one gun.

She came back into the kitchen with the jeans on. She had another gun in her hand. Phillip started to say something, but then thought better of it. Instead, he asked, "Do you have someone we can call?"

Laurie said, "Yes. Yes, my mother."

Laurie dialed Mrs. Wasserman on the phone. Luckily, her mother was at home.

"Oh Momma, I've done something terrible! I've done something terrible! I shot someone Momma!"

Dann became hysterical on the phone, releasing a torrent of bawling and nonsense. Phillip grabbed the phone from her, tried to explain that, as Laurie had told them, a man had raped her and she had shot him in self-defense. Mrs. Wasserman was helpless on the other end of the line.

No, she could not come and get Laurie. She did not have a car.

At this time, Mr. Andrew arrived home from work. He was predictably not amused.

"Okay young lady, give us the gun. C'mon…"

Laurie, informed that she could contact her mother again, became less paranoid. She did, and Mrs. Andrews quickly slipped away, while her husband argued with Dann about putting down her gun.

She ordered Mr. Andrews out of the house, but commanded that their son Phillip stay behind as a hostage. At some point, Dann realized that the game was up, because she shot Phillip Andrews in the chest, and then ran upstairs.

While Phillip Andrews crawled out the back door to safety, (an ambulance that had pulled up immediately cared for him), police surrounded the house and a SWAT team went inside. Laurie's mother was outside with the police and a bullhorn, trying to get her daughter's attention.

She was too late.

Police found Laurie Dann in an upstairs bedroom.

She had shot herself in the mouth.

***

Although Laurie killed one boy, all other victims managed to survive the attacks, though at great physical and psychological cost. Several groups of parents went on to campaign for tighter gun control laws, and a greater ability on behalf of the courts to commit the mentally ill when they obviously need it badly.

We could add a bit further to this chapter, but we feel that anyone interested in further research can do so themselves. The present author believes he has said enough about this particular case, and that the chapter is finished best by asserting the indisputable fact that Laurie Dann was a very curious girl.

Jeffrey Dahmer

"I have to question whether there is an evil force in the world and whether or not I have been influenced by it."

~Jeffrey Dahmer

The police officers that entered Apartment 213 at 924 North 25th Street in Milwaukee, Wisconsin, that day in 1991 must have thought they had entered a doorway into hell.

Inside, they found the remains of a number of butchered young men: torsos, heads in freezers, pictures of the butchered kept so the killer could gloat over them later. The remains, one officer noted, "were not inconsistent with cannibalism."

The police had, initially, been drawn to the place when they saw a handcuffed, nude African American male running down the street. That victim would prove to be one Tracy Edwards, a man whom the resident of the apartment had befriended only recently. Edwards accompanied the resident back to his place under the pretext of a homosexual liaison.

The owner of the apartment, a man whose name would soon explode in the international media as a byword of murder and degeneracy, was one Jeffrey Lionel Dahmer, an employee of the Ambrosia Chocolate Factory. And, apparently, a serial killer.

***

Jeffrey Dahmer was born May 21, 1960, to a middle class couple with marital problems. The mother, at least, suffered from nervous disorders, and the father was "aloof," to characterize him charitably. At first, the young boy evinced no serious maladaptive traits. Yet, as fate would have it, after a move to Bath Township Ohio by the family, Jeffrey would experience the awful fate of being sexually molested by an older adult relative. It was this sorry happening that many think led, later on, to the monstrous horrors that were to be perpetrated by the young Dahmer.

Jeffrey's parents inevitably bickered, and it was this bickering that seemed to lead to the dark impulses that would blossom into Jeffrey's first experiments in butchery. Jeffrey began to collect road kill, and eventually snuff out the lives of living animals, all to satisfy a burning curiosity about the inner workings of things. It could be argued that at this time, his inner cravings became confused with sexual excitement, with the need to be alone, solitary, and to pursue his own selfish desires.

Jeffrey would bleach chicken bones, decapitate rodents, and make macabre attempts to stuff animals for preservation, once going so far as to mount a dog's head on a stake. This could not have done anything but alarm the boy's parents (and neighbors who became increasingly privy to his disturbing doings), but, nonetheless, no one came forward to intervene, or suggest that the increasingly troubled boy should seek psychiatric treatment. Jeffrey was allowed to delve deep into his grotesque hobby, and his fantasies at this time became heated homosexual meditations, often tinged with an air of necrophilia.

Lionel and Joyce Dahmer finally divorced by 1978, and both of them left the home they had shared for many years, leaving young Jeffrey to his own twisted devices. By this point, he had discovered that he was an alcoholic, and had been drinking secretly for years, a habit that would arguably be one of the greatest contributing factors to his downfall. Left alone, Jeffrey, and the twisted thoughts that brooded inside of his twisted skull, could be given free reign to grow until, finally, they exploded in a horrific incident that was to be the first of many.

***

Jeffrey turned the car to the shoulder of the road. The young man standing there with his thumb out seemed awful grateful to be getting a lift.

"Hey man, thanks!" said the young man, getting into the passenger seat of the car. The young man driving was tall, blond, and not bad looking.

"So where you headed?"

"Well, tell you the truth, man, I really got no destination in mind... I'm just kind of new at this whole game, I guess."

The two drove on in silence for a moment before the young man said, "Hey, why don't we go back to my place for a little bit. You look kind of thirsty. Feel like a beer?"

The young hitch hiker looked over at the driver nervously. He didn't know if he should trust the guy or not, but a beer, and maybe a sandwich sounded good right about now. And besides, where else did he have to go?

"Sure. I guess that would be okay."

The driver smiled. Perhaps in his mind he hadn't really thought through what he was going to do, or perhaps he had only a subconscious inclination, an inner demon urging him forward. Whatever the case, in time they pulled up to the young man's house.

"My parents are gone."

He said this finally and flatly, as if it cost him a little pain to admit.

"Really? When will they be back?"

"I don't know... I mean, they go away sometimes. Maybe they won't come back at all. We have the place all to ourselves."

They parked, and the men got out. The young driver led the hitchhiker into the house through the garage. Inside all was quiet, if somewhat squalid from the poor housekeeping of the young man.

The hitchhiker sat down. He had left his pack in the car. The young man went to fix them some sandwiches, talking in a cool, low, casual voice the whole time.

"So what's your story man? You got a girlfriend or go to college or something? Geez you look pretty young. Of course, looks can be deceiving."

The young man spread mayo across two slices of bread, got a plate, put the sandwiches and some chips on it, and went into the fridge for some beer. The young hitchhiker was nervously quiet, and was unsure about how much information he wanted to give to this guy.

"Oh, man, I'm just passing through you know," he said. "Just trying to see the width and breadth of this great big country of ours." He said this and laughed, but his laugh was nervous. The tall blond guy was charming enough, but there was something about him that seemed not to be quite right somehow. A sort of weird, detached, low-key creepiness that rested just below the surface of the charm. He was a strange fish alright.

The young hitch hiker took the sandwich and devoured it greedily. He then drank the beer in a few gulps, and feeling a little bit better, settled back into a chair in the living room, and faced his host.

"Hey man, you want to watch some TV?" he suggested. It had been awhile since he had been able to catch any of his favorite shows.

"Why don't we just talk?" said the tall blond guy, whose name was Jeff. "I get so awful lonely here sometimes. It's so quiet in this house with everyone gone. I'm sure you understand."

The hitchhiker looked a little dismayed, and realized how strange his new friend was.

"Okay," he said. "We can talk. What do you want to talk about?"

Invariably, Jeff wanted to talk about his peculiar hobbies, his loneliness, his weird fascination with the occult, and, most of all, he slowly admitted his attraction to males.

All of this made the hitchhiker more and more uncomfortable. But what could he do? He didn't feel like he could just get up and walk out, and even if he did, where in the world would he go?

This place seemed like it was out in the middle of nowhere.

"Hey man, I don't swing that way, okay."

"Have you ever thought about it?"

"No. And I'm not pissed or anything but I'm telling you, just so you know."

"Okay, no problem. Hey, you want another beer? Wait, I've got something even better."

Jeffrey brought out beer and liquor, and proceeded to get his young guest more than a little drunk. He continued his slow, calm, casual conversation. He was liking this, this feeling of…togetherness. It seemed like his depression was lifting some, and loneliness was far from his mind.

The young hitcher talked about his family, how he and his old man never got along, about his girlfriend and the problems they had. He became progressively more drunk, and Jeff liked that. It made him more pliable, more easy-going. Jeff could feel himself starting to get excited.

"Man, you're ripped Steve. Man, I've seen a lot of guys with muscles, but, man, you are one ripped mother&%$#%!"

Jeff was drunk now, too. But he was clearheaded (or at least felt clearheaded) enough to control the situation.

"Hey Steven man, why don't you let me get a picture of you with your shirt off?"

Steven laughed, looked at Jeffrey with a knowing little look, and was too drunk to be intimidated at this point. Besides, he felt, at this point, strong enough to knock Jeffrey through the wall if he tried anything. He slurred out, "Sure thing, man..." and stood up, unbuttoning his shirt and swaying drunkenly in the living room.

Jeffrey couldn't find the camera at first.

When he did, he realized that he didn't have any film left.

Well, that was okay. He had other ideas now.

"Say Steve, I got a weight bench down in the basement man. How's about seeing how much you and I can lift?"

"S'okay but, hey man, I gotta be getting' on soon, y'know?'

Steven was slurring his speech a little, but was sobering up enough to realize that it was now nearly dark, and he wanted to be off soon. However, he followed Jeff down into the basement, and sure enough, there were they gray remains of an old weight-lifting bench in the center of the floor.

"Ish shure is nice down here, maan... I mean, you shleep down here, Jeff?"

"Sometimes." Jeff smiled. He put the barbells on the weight bar and laid down. He lifted.

Steven was surprised at just how strong Jeffrey was. He had the strength of an ox it seemed, even though he sure didn't look it.

Jeffrey got up, staggering a little. He was huffing and puffing and his face was red. He said, "Okay Steven, my ripped man... Now it's your turn."

Steven laid down, realizing he was too drunk to be lifting weights. He struggled against the bar, but he was only able to do a little of what Jeff had.

"Oh man, I am so out of shape, man. Hey man, that's it."

Steven sat up on the bench and sighed. He wanted to go. For some reason this was all of a sudden the last place he wanted to crash.

"I need to get back on the road man. You give me a lift? I really need to go."

Jeff didn't like the sound of that.

His face fell.

He felt the black rage grow inside of him.

Steve was his friend, and now Steve was going to desert him. Just like his parents had. Just like everyone always had.

Jeff hated being alone.

He felt the black demon of despair well up in him, his animal self screaming in the darkness from some place he could barely understand. He said, in a low, toneless, eerie voice, "You can't leave me, Steven. You're going to stay here tonight. With me."

Steven felt his face go slack. Even though he was still partially drunk, he could see that he was in a hairy predicament. He felt angry at being told what he was going to do.

"*%$& you, Jeff. I'm not your punk."

He stood up from the weight bench and started to walk up the basement stairs.

Jeffrey felt the lights go out.

He pounced forward.

He brought the weight-lifting bar down on Steven's head again and again. Steven dropped to the concrete floor, blood flowing out in a pool beneath him.

Jeffrey realized he wasn't dead.

He grabbed Steven by the throat and began to strangle him.

He could feel the body squirm and thrash beneath him.

He had never felt so sexually excited in his entire life.

Later, he could do some real experimenting, as he dismembered Steven in the bathtub, stuffing the various pieces of him in black garbage bags and burying them in the backyard later.

***

It was after this crime that Jeffrey made a half-hearted attempt to go to college, enrolling in Ohio State University. The class clown in him (a roll that he had first assumed in grade school) came out though, and scuttled whatever hope he might have possessed in getting a degree. In short time, he withdrew from classes, as he was drinking too heavily to attend.

His father, freshly divorced from his mother, now reentered Jeffrey's life, and convinced the young man that his best prospect would be to pursue a career in the military. Jeffrey signed up, and was stationed in Germany.

Alas, his drinking got to him here too…and perhaps, the slumbering, sick urges also reared their demonic head again, as a string of unsolved murders plagued the area that Jeffrey was stationed in. Of course, there is no hard proof that Dahmer actually committed any of these crimes, but the fact that he was living in the same area while they were being committed still troubles researchers to this day.

Jeffrey drank himself out of the military after two years, receiving a dishonorable discharge, and came home seeming to have no prospects for the future. He did not return to Ohio, but instead was permitted to stay with his grandmother in the city of his birth, the West Allis suburb of Milwaukee. Here Jeffrey was given his own room, and his grandmother was more than accommodating in giving her grandson ample breathing space to do as he pleased.

It was then that the temporarily slumbering demons began to torment the young alcoholic again, and he made a spiritual pilgrimage back to the scene of his first murder, exhuming the trash bags containing the rotting, dismembered pieces of Steven Hicks, and, inexplicably, hammering them into bits with a sledge hammer before scattering the remains in the nearby woods. We can only assume Dahmer took this unusual step as a precaution, and also to relive the thrill he must have felt at committing that first, mad crime.

He finally secured employment at the Ambrosia Chocolate Factory, of which one co-worker stated, "Jeff was the kind of guy that could spend his lunch break eating alone, staring at the wall." When he wasn't doing this, he was frequently lost in the world of the heavy metal music he listened to on his headphones in his spare time. His favorite group was reportedly Black Sabbath.

(Some have described Dahmer as entering an almost trance-like state when he listened to his music, as if it effected him in a way that was altogether more visceral than what one might expect from a casual listener. We can only guess at the bizarre, horrific imagery he was conjuring forth as he listened to the heavy, gloomy rock.)

It was at this time that his slumbering homosexuality began to blossom and take shape, and Jeffrey became a fixture at local gay bars and hangouts. This singles meat market would prove to be a happy hunting ground for the dangerously blossoming psychopath.

Jeffrey was arrested at an outdoor festival in Milwaukee for "indecent exposure," but no charge was ever filed against him and the police might have put it off to a drunken prank. Four years later, in 1986, Jeffrey ran afoul of the law once again when two boys complained that a man answering Dahmer's description had exposed himself and proceeded to masturbate in front of them. Dahmer was remembered by the police from his earlier incident, and this time taken to court, where he rated a sentence of "disorderly conduct" and was given a year-long suspended sentence. He was also ordered to undergo psychiatric counseling.

On September 15th of 1987, Dahmer, good and drunk, escorted a young male named Steven Tuomi to a local hotel for the purposes of a sexual encounter. When Dahmer awoke the next day, he unaccountably found Tuomi dead with blood covering his mouth. This was his second murder, but he later denied having had any memory of what precisely occurred during his "blackout."

He stuffed the body into a large suitcase, and took it back to his grandmother's house. He later admitted to having sex with the corpse, masturbating over it, and then dismembering it, disposing of the various body parts in several garbage cans.

His next victim was Jamie Doxtator, a dark-complected Native American boy he met at one of the gay bars. He took Jamie home with him under the pretense of posing for some pictures, offering him fifty dollars. He got him back to his room, drugged his beer, and then killed him. He later admitted to drinking the blood and licking the flesh, perhaps here infusing his sick sexual fantasies with the element of cannibalism that would later become his defining hallmark. He also collected the skull and some of the body parts of Jamie Doxtator.

Next, a young Mexican man named Richard Guerrero became victim number four. Dahmer invited him back to his room under the same pretence, finished him off with drugs, stabbed him, dismembered him, and cut up his biceps and muscles to put in his freezer. He later admitted he ate them.

Of course, with all the body parts he was collecting it was inevitable that weird smells came wafting up from Jeffrey's basement room, and even his tolerant grandmother found she was nearing the end of her rope with the young reprobate. She kindly suggested that it was time for Jeffrey to get his own place, so he could conduct his weird, smelly "experiments" (as he claimed they were) on his own.

Jeffrey did just this, and discovered a new freedom to practice his macabre butchery that he had hitherto not known.

Jeffrey was soon up to his old tricks again. He hired fourteen-year-old Sounth Sinthasomphone to pose for some pictures, and lured the young boy back to his apartment, where he drugged him, fondled his genitals, and attempted to rape him. The boy later awoke in a heavily drugged state, and, making his way back home, found his parents horrified at what had happened to him. It was a quick trip to the police station later where Sinthasomphone fingered Dahmer as the culprit, and Jeffrey was arrested on serious charges this time.

Dahmer plead guilty to second-degree sexual assault and was released to await sentencing. He went back to his grandmother's house, where he lured yet another man, Anthony Sears, to his basement room of murder.

Sears was an aspiring male model, so the offer of posing for pictures was not something that unduly troubled him. Jeffrey drugged, stabbed, and dismembered him, indulging in necrophilia and eating parts of Sears' body. He then boiled the flesh off the skull, painted it grey so that it would look like a medical novelty, and kept it as a memento. It would later be found in Apartment 213 with a collection of others.

Jeffrey was examined by three psychiatrists for the sexual molestation charge, who each admitted that he was an evasive and resistant subject, and that he was fundamentally incapable of admitting to the fact that he had even done any wrong – except that he had chosen a boy that was "too young."

Dahmer pleaded for leniency, and claimed that the only thing that kept him even remotely stable was his job at Ambrosia Chocolate Factory.

He told the court:

> The one thing I have in my mind that is stable and gives me a sense of pride is my job... I've come very close to losing it because of my actions, for which I take full responsibility. All I can do is beg you, please spare my job. Please give me a chance to show that I can tread the straight and narrow and not get involved in any situation like this ever again. This enticing a child was the climax of my idiocy.

Indeed, it was not, as he claimed, the "climax of his idiocy;" it was his first taste of incarceration, as he was sentenced to one year in the house of corrections and a work release program that allowed him to work at Ambrosia by day and return to the institution at night. Dahmer's father Lionel actually begged the judge to keep his son locked away until he could get help, but, such were the circumstances that Dahmer soon found himself a free man again.

He returned to his grandmother's for awhile, and from there to Apartment 213, where he would go on to commit his final bloody marathon of butchery.

He committed twelve more murders while living at Apartment 213.

Edward Smith, Raymond Smith, Ricky Lee Beeks, Ernest Miller, and David Thomas followed in short order. Dahmer would ply these unfortunates (invariably they were young African American men, the sort Dahmer was attracted to) with drugged food or liquor, strangle them, cut them to pieces, often photograph himself having sex with the corpses, save the body parts for eating later (he employed special seasonings for taste) and then dissolve the remains that he didn't keep in an acid solution in his bathtub. These would invariably develop into a scum that could easily be flushed down the toilet.

Dahmer would later also employ several plastic barrels of acid for the same purpose.

As Dahmer descended into madness, his bizarre obsession with the occult and obtaining power caused him to erect an alter with black candles, skulls, a griffon, and incense in one corner of the room. He admitted later to using body parts in his private rituals, to see if he could summon demonic energy to aid him socially and financially.

His favorite viewing at this time were the movies *Exorcist 3* and *Faces of Death*. Dahmer had broken through the thin layer of sanity holding him tethered tenuously to the world of living men. Now, he was a full-on medieval monster, an ogre with his own private world of butchery and voodoo, ritual, and cannibalistic rite. He was now a modern savage, let loose from the restraint that divides men from animals.

However, he had to keep the mask of sanity firmly in place, at least in so much as he needed to walk the streets and go to work and continue to put up the pretence of living and being an actual human. He did this quite successfully for a long while.

***

One of the most remarkable activities Dahmer engaged in was his bizarre obsession with creating living zombies out of his victims – sex slaves that he could keep and command at will for his sick amusement. To this end, he practiced doing drill bit lobotomies, pouring acid into the cranial wounds and hoping to have enough of the brain eaten away by this horrific practice to have a real, live compliant "zombie" to satisfy his whims and stave off his loneliness. Of course, all of these victims died immediately.

***

The young boy stumbled, nude, down the street. There was blood running down his face.

Nichole and Sandra went out to see what was the matter with the boy.

"Hey man, are you okay? Are you gonna be okay? Man, what happened to you? You look like somebody done a number on you."

The boy collapsed in the road. They couldn't understand a thing he was saying. He was Laotian, and the two girls realized he probably didn't speak any English.

"Hey man, do you speak English at all? Man, I think we need to call an ambulance, Sandra. He looks like he's bleedin' bad. Man, somebody messed him up."

Suddenly, a cop car turned down the street, at one of the girls stayed with the boy while the other went to flag down the cop.

"Officer! Officer! We got a boy over here looks like somebody has messed him up bad!"

The cop drove over to where Nicole was bent over the boy. He tried to help the kid up onto his feet, but he seemed…drunk. The cop didn't know. Anyway, the kid had a little blood on him and was nude. The cop thought he had better take him in.

He asked the kid where he lived.

The only thing the confused boy could do was point to the nearby apartment block wherein he had come from. Apartment 213. Jeffrey's home.

Jeffrey suddenly appeared, held up his hands, and said, "Officer, this is my boyfriend. He's an adult. He doesn't speak much English though. Sorry. About all this… I guess we just had too much to drink tonight and things got carried away. I'll take him home, put him to bed."

The cops accepted Dahmer's story and handed the inebriated boy back over to him. The two girls were incredulous.

"What! You aren't going to let him go back with that guy, are you?"

"I can't believe this! Officer, this boy needs to get to a hospital!"

One of the cops turned angrily to the two girls and said, "I don't want any lip out of you two, or you'll be taking a ride in the back of the car to the station!"

Jeffrey took Konerak Sinthasomphone back to his apartment and killed him. In an instant of monstrous irony, it was Konerak's older brother Sounth Sinthasomphone who had escaped Dahmer's clutches two years earlier.

On the way back to the station, the cops made racist jokes about being "deloused."

His latest brush with the law sent Jeffrey into a final murderous rage, and he quickly dispatched several more victims over the next two months.

These would include Matt Turner, Jeremiah Weinberger, Oliver Lacy, and Joseph Bradehoft. By July 22nd, however, Dahmer's luck had finally run its course.

***

The other tenants were complaining about the smell coming out of 213. It was really foul. Dahmer, when confronted about the putrescent smell wafting from his gloomy abode, variously gave the excuse of faulty plumbing or "meat" that had gone bad when his freezer malfunctioned. He promised he would do something about it.

Of course, there was rotten meat in Dahmer's apartment – human meat. The rancid smell he exuded was not, however, what finally led to the undoing of Jeffrey Dahmer.

That would be his invite of one Tracy Edwards back to his flat for a few drinks.

Edwards was found by Milwaukee police bloody, incoherent, and stumbling down the street with a pair of handcuffs dangling from one wrist. He explained as best he could that he had been invited by a man named Jeff back to his apartment for a few drinks, and that the guy had handcuffed him and tried to kill him. Even though he had been drugged, Edwards had the presence of mind to lead the police back to Apartment 213, where Dahmer came to the door with a ready-made excuse. He told the cops that Edwards was his homosexual lover, and that they had just been playing a "kinky game" that Edwards had objected to when he had punched Jeffrey and run out the door.

The cops weren't buying it.

There was a horrible smell coming out of Jeffrey's apartment, a smell that alerted them right away.

Dahmer seemed, for his part, not to be able to comprehend the seriousness of what was occurring. He invited the cops inside, where they quickly saw the photos of mutilated men adorning the walls in the bedroom.

They acted in concert to subdue and handcuff Dahmer, who behaved as if he was in a "religious trance."

They discovered a head in the icebox.

They discovered human hands in a pot on the stove.

They found jars of yellow liquid in which floated severed male organs.

There were, likewise, frozen bags of human flesh in the freezer.

The cops were sickened beyond belief. For Jeffrey Dahmer, the game was up.

***

The resultant trial created a firestorm of publicity, making Dahmer a household name overnight. He openly confessed to thirteen years of murder, and cops discovered what would be the remains of seventeen men Jeffrey had slaughtered. His crimes were so shocking, so beyond the pale of normal decency, that they easily recalled and greatly surpassed the crimes of the degenerate Ed Gein from decades earlier.

The media sensation became the stuff of talk shows, cheap paperbacks, low budget movies, and even comic books and trading cards. Jeff, it would seem, had found lasting infamy.

In the end he was convicted and sentenced to fifteen consecutive life terms, totaling nine hundred years. Ironically, it was Jeffrey's destiny to die as violently as he had made his many victims die. Not long after being sentenced to his life without parole, Dahmer (who had embraced religion while behind bars, and who refused any offers of protective custody in spite of the fact that many inmates wanted to see him dead) was beaten to death with a bar from a prison weight set while he was cleaning a toilet.

The killer was a schizophrenic inmate named Christopher Scarver, a man who believed he was the "Son of God."

(If so, he must have thought it was high time to call Jeffrey home.)

Dahmer died in 1992. Attempts to have his brain preserved for study by doctors were quashed by legal proceedings from his father, who went on to write an autobiography about raising young Jeffrey Dahmer.

Hollywood continues to crank out movies about the cannibal killer.

One supposes there is no accounting for taste.

Herb Baumeister

The story of Herbert Baumeister is, as far as serial killers are concerned, fairly typical: Baumeister was an Indianapolis businessman, father, successful citizen, and psychopathic sexual sadist who lured an estimated eleven young men to his estate at Fox Hollow Farms before strangling them in the basement swimming pool and burying their bodies on his sprawling property. These young men were invariably homosexuals pulled from the various gay bars in Indianapolis that Baumeister frequented.

One of the most puzzling aspects of the Baumesiter case was the fact that the man had been giving off warning signs about his various abnormalities since he was a child – yet, each and everyone associated with him had chosen to ignore these warning signs. It was a disregard that was to prove fatal for almost a dozen victims.

Herbert Baumeister was born the son of a doctor, and it was this influential and privileged upbringing that was to secure for him a job on the *Indianapolis Star* newspaper later in life.

As a boy, Herb was given to doing and thinking strange things, confessing to a classmate that he sometimes wondered what it would be like to taste urine. He sometimes committed strange pranks, too, like leaving a dead crow on the desk of a teacher.

Herb never dated the girls. Most assumed he didn't much care for them.

By young adulthood, he was drifting in and out of college; he seemed aimless, without direction. Most did not know that he had already been diagnosed as a schizophrenic when he was a child.

His father helped him secure employment, first at the Indianapolis Star, where he was thought of as a well-spoken, eager, well-dressed young man who, unfortunately, never quite took to the job as copyboy.

Once Herb picked his young friends up for an IU basketball game while driving a hearse. While Herb obviously found the prank hilarious, his friends were nonplussed. Herb Baumeister, they decided, was a real oddball.

He didn't fare much better at the Department of Motor Vehicles where he, at times, paid back whatever grief given to him by his employer by urinating on the man's desk. Amazingly, although it was "no secret" that it was Herb who was responsible, he was able to pull off this repulsive stunt twice before he was fired. Before that, he troubled his co-workers by sending them all a photo of himself dressed in drag.

Herb was, to put it mildly, already an unusual cat by anyone's standards.

In 1971, Herb married Julie, a high school journalism instructor. Both seemed to share equal ideas about what they wanted out of life: Both wanted to be wealthy, own their own business, and live the "American dream."

Herb went to work for a thrift store for three years while Julie took the role of principal breadwinner. Herb was very talented at managing his new position, and, in time, with a $4,000 dollar loan, was able to open his own establishment, the "Sav-A-Lot" store, in conjunction with a local children's charity.

At first, the store was top-notch, as far as such stores go, and Herb soon found himself making money hand over fist. He was successful enough in his first year to open up a second location, buy a posh new home (although those who entered were convinced that rags-to-riches couple had no sense of taste) and count himself among the up-and-coming young businessmen of 1991.

The new home was a Tudor-style house on eighteen acres of property in the posh Westfield district. It was, as far as Herb Baumeister and his needs were concerned, as close to paradise as one can possibly get. For others it would become a living hell.

***

The marriage, which produced several children, was nonetheless oddly sexless; Herb did not like for his wife to see him naked, and she never did, completely. Otherwise, he was distant most of the time, except for when important decisions had to be made. Then, he ruled the roost. His wife deferred to his judgment in all things.

Despite the posh house, the money, and the three children, Julie was want to split from Herb from time to time, or take the children to see Grandma Baumeister for extended visits. Herb seemed to have been a very secretive, unpleasant chap to have been around, and obviously, while she didn't wish to break completely away from him, Julie decided that she really didn't much enjoy his company.

One very telling incident occurred when one of Baumeister's sons dug up a full human skeleton in the backyard while he was playing. While this would have been enough to send most people packing to the police, Herb shrugged off his wife's terrified outrage by proclaiming that it had been "one of my father's dissecting skeletons" that had been stashed in the garage, and that when Herb decided it was in the way he had dragged it out back and buried it.

Unbelievably, Julie Baumeister bought this bizarre explanation.

***

A number of young homosexual men had been disappearing from local gay bars in the Indianapolis area. One such man was named Broussard, and his mother immediately sought the help of a local private detective named Vandagriff. Mr. Vandagriff initially thought that Mr. Broussard might simply have vanished to a place that was more friendly and accepting of the homosexual lifestyle. He soon began to doubt this conclusion, however, when he found that a local police detective, Mary Wilson, was investigating the disappearances of young gay men from several bars in the area. Another point of interest for Vandagriff came in the form of a gay publication that featured the story of a young man named Roger Goodlet, who had likewise disappeared while frequenting an Indianapolis bar. The words of the mother reprinted in the article and the story itself felt a bit too familiar to Vandagriff, who felt, suddenly, that they might have serial killer of young gay men working in Indianapolis.

He took his information to Detective Mary Wilson on the Indianapolis Police Department who was investigating the disappearances of four young gay men, all under the same mysterious circumstances. Vandagriff had recently been put into contact with a young man named "Tony," who had learned of him by phoning his friend Roger Goodlet's mother. Vandagriff took "Tony" to speak with Mary Wilson, who felt she might just have found the key witness she needed.

"Tony" was convinced that he had spent the night with a man that might be responsible for the disappearance of Roger Goodlet and so many other young gay men. He eagerly told his story.

***

It was at the 501 Club where Tony had first set eyes upon the man he now believed to be a killer.

Tony had first noticed the man because he was staring, fixedly, at the Missing Persons poster behind the bar at the club. Tony was certain he was onto something when he introduced himself to the tall, silent man. The man told him that his name was "Brian Smart."

Brian claimed not to know anything about Roger Goodlet, and claimed never to have even met the man, but came onto Tony pretty quick.

"I'm a landscape artist. I'm currently living in an empty house... owners are gone and I'm supposed to get the grounds in shape before they come back. Hey, want to come back to my place for a drink?"

Tony accompanied Brian Smart back to his car, a Buick, and let Brian drive him out to "rich people's country," a rolling expanse of suburbs that included split-rail fences and horse farms. Brian kept the direction they were driving in his mind as best he could, and remembered there was a sign in front of the house they parked at, a sign that included the word "farm" in its title.

The place was undoubtedly a mansion, and Brian led Tony through a side entrance and into a set of lavishly, if tastelessly, furnished rooms, until they got to a set of stairs.

Apparently, the electricity was cut off everywhere in the house except for the basement. Or so Brian told Tony.

Brian led Tony down the basement steps.

Tony did a double-take.

There were a number of...mannequins posed in strange positions all over the place. Apparently, these were some of Brian's less lively "companions."

The sight was odd, and threw Tony off, but the basement did include a large swimming pool, and it was no time before the two men had stripped down and availed themselves of the facility.

"Man, this is great! It must be awesome having a pool all to yourself..."

"Yeah, it's not too bad. I like it. Hey, let me make you that drink."

Tony said, "No, that's okay man. I don't think I really need it. I had a lot to drink at the bar, you know. Need to sober up a bit."

"Oh come on, Tony. One little drinky-poo? Never hurt anyone. Get you good and loosened up. Make you more talkative."

"Hey, you seem to be able to talk enough for the both of us," said Tony, but he noticed that Brian was getting very tense.

"Well, okay man, whatever. I need to loosen up a little. Hold on." And Brian disappeared for a few moments.

When he came back, he seemed as if he had just snorted some coke. He was jabbering a mile a minute, and seemed happy as hell again. Tony got out of the pool with a sense of mounting unease.

"Hey man, I just learned a neat new trick. You know what it is? I learned that if you strangle someone while you're having sex, it's... incredible. It's a total rush for them! It's like, the greatest orgasm in the world!"

"Man, quit %$#&-ing around..."

"No! No, really, you see, you just close off these two veins here..." Brian pointed to the arteries in his neck.

"You...you stop before, you know...It's just a game man."

Then Brian said: "Do it to me."

He started to fix a length of garden hose into a noose, and then lay down on a nearby couch. Tony, numb with fear, began to do as Brian directed, strangling him while he masturbated. Brian loved it, and when he was finished he said, "Now, I'll do it to you. Lie down."

Tony, still not quite believing what he was doing, did as Brian instructed. Suddenly, the garden hose was around his neck, and Brian was choking...hard.

Tony pretended to lose consciousness.

Brian relented.

Tony opened his eyes, and Brian became angry, saying, "You scared the shit out of me, man! You know you can die doing this! There have been accidents!"

Then Tony did something unbelievably bold. He asked, "Is that what happened to Roger Goodlet? Was he one of your 'accidents?' Have there been others?"

But Brian simply grinned at him and tossed the hose away, bored with the game now. He passed out on the couch, whether from a combination of booze and drugs, or just through sheer exhaustion, was unclear.

Tony had a chance to go through the rest of the house, quickly. He very soon surmised that Brian Smart was lying.

He went back down to the basement and picked up Brian Smart's pants. He wanted to see if there was a wallet. Get some ID.

Brian rolled over and snorted. Apparently, the old monster was waking up.

Tony lost his chance. For now.

***

Brian told Tony he was a "good sport" that "really knew how to play," and drove him back to town. He made Tony promise to meet him again at the 501 Club next week.

Vandagriff was careful to post a man at the bar when Tony showed up to keep his date with "Brian Smart." The detective was eager to see if this particular man could be linked to the disappearances of young gay men in the area, and felt that, most likely, Brian Smart was the culprit they were looking for. Unfortunately, Brian Smart failed to put in an appearance that night.

***

Vandagriff and police detective Mary Wilson didn't have much to go on.

The directions that Tony was able to give to "Brian Smart's" house were very vague, placing it in a rough position somewhere in one of two exclusive suburbs in Hamilton County. The best that Tony could remember was that the place had the word "Farms" somewhere in the title.

The investigation stalled for a year.

In the meantime, Herb Baumeister gave the appearance of a man who was quickly coming unglued. His marriage was beginning to go South, his wife growing weary of his distant, sexless lack of affection, and his Sav-A-Lot stores were fast losing customers. Herb was proving to be a drunken, tyrannical boss, and the earlier competence he had shown as a manager was fast slipping from him. The stores soon became sloppy, and employees began to complain of excessive hours and cruel policies. Herb would steal out of the office for a quick nip of booze, and return, ranting and raving. It was a hopeless mess.

It was a year later that Herb felt confident enough to get back out into the gay scene. His first stop was a place called the Varsity Lounge.

As luck would have it (but not for Herb), Tony just happened to be there that night.

Tony excitedly remembered his previous encounter with Brian Smart.

He made sure to approach Brian, strike up a conversation, and, most importantly, follow him out to the parking lot and get his license plate numbers.

When Mary Wilson ran the numbers later, they proved to the vehicle belonged to a man named Herbert Baumeister.

Bingo!

***

The police approached Herb Baumeister at work to let him know they suspected him of being involved in the disappearances of the young men. Herb stonewalled, and said they would have to contact his lawyer. They then approached Julie Baumeister, knowing that she was the only other person who could grant police the legal power to search Fox Hollow Farms without a warrant. She looked stunned as she was told the reason for the search, but she, too, refused to cooperate.

It took six months to get the warrant. Detective Vandagriff later guessed it was because Mary Wilson was an Indianapolis Police Detective and didn't have the jurisdiction to operate in Hamilton County suburbs. Also, that the State Police had an attitude that the affluent people of Carmel were "rich, therefore above suspicion." In short: they thought it would all be for not.

By the time that police were ready to search Fox Hollow Farms, Julie Baumeister had already filed for divorce. She informed her lawyer that he should inform Mary Wilson that it was fine that she search the residence. Also, she informed them of the bones she had found in the yard...

***

Herb had taken their youngest son to Lake Wawasee to see relatives. This provided the perfect opportunity for police to search the grounds while he was away. It did, however present a problem for Julie, as to how to get her young son back from Baumeister in case the police actually DID find something. This would eventually be accomplished by police, before Herb even knew anything about the search that was going on back at Fox Hollow Farms.

The area beyond the back porch proved to be littered in charred bones, pieces of teeth, and other detritus that Mary Wilson was sure were human remains. The county investigators were not so sure, and believed that the remains could possibly be animal remains. Whether they were human or animal, they certainly seemed to be finding a lot of them...

It was only later, after a report from a forensic anthropologist confirmed for them that the remains were, indeed, those of burnt human bodies, that the county investigators could wrap their heads around what they were finding. In all there seemed to be the bodies of, at least, a dozen young men.

Detectives assembled outside Fox Hollow Farms, along with the forensic pathologist that had originally identified the remains as human. As they went, they dropped an orange flag whenever they found another fragment of bone, eventually dropping over a hundred.

Inside the Baumeister residence, the police found much what they expected from Tony's description. They also found a video camera, which they suspected had been used by Herb to record the killings for his later enjoyment.

The police were now certain that they had a serial killer on their hands. Herb, apparently, had waited until his family was away visiting his mother to seduce, strangle, and then burn the bodies of young gay men.

On property adjacent to Fox Hollow, in an old drainage ditch, they found a plethora of bones and teeth sticking up out of the mud. Inside this ditch were the remains of numerous victims.

Once all remains were finally collected, police realized they had the bodies of eleven men on their hands. Only five of the victims were ever identified.

And what of Herb? Police had managed to obtain a court order to have his son brought back home before the investigation commenced and the bodies were discovered, but, having no reason at the time to detain Herb, he was allowed to venture into Ontario Canada, to Piney Provincial Park. It was here, on July 3rd of 1996, he committed suicide, blowing his brains out.

Herb, though never convicted, is suspected in the deaths of twenty men, an additional nine being victims of the I-70 slayer who was never apprehended. According to Wikipedia, an online resource, Herb is also suspected of foul play in the death of an older brother who met his fate under mysterious circumstances in Texas.

Thus ends the strange saga of Herb Baumeister.

The Wages of Sin

They don't think they're too smart or desperate
They know that the law always wins.
They've been shot at before;
But they do not ignore,
That death is the wages of sin.

~Bonnie Parker

Our last chapter brings us to the logical conclusion to be drawn from the stories that make up the present volume: Crime does not pay.

America currently incarcerates an estimated 2.2 million people, more than any other country in the world. Even with the sweeping, modern reforms and the focus on human rights, prisons are still harsh, horrible, and sometimes deadly places. An estimated 20,000 men and boys can expect to be sexually assaulted while behind bars every year. Seventy-five inmates were murdered in correctional institutions in 2005.

Riots and violence can break out at any time.

This is not to mention the fact that the rates for HIV (the virus believed to be responsible for the spread of AIDS) as well as deadly Hepatitis C, are four times higher in the prison population than in general society. (Hepatitis C is said to be able to live on metal surfaces for up to six weeks.)

Besides the dangers of disease, physical, and sexual assault, the inmate is forced to deal with an environment that is psychologically devastating, confined long hours in a cage with someone who may be actively hostile to him, surrounded by aggressive, psychotic inmates and staff who are, unfortunately, sometimes as criminally corrupt as the convicts they are paid to police. (Note: this is not intended as a slur against the fine men and women who are legitimate correctional officers, and who do a job that is indispensable to the public at large. My father was one such officer. I am simply stating an unfortunate fact.)

They are stripped of most of their rights and all of their dignity, separated from their families for years and sometimes forever, cut off from any tendrils of normality that once held them somewhat mentally in check. Often they are drawn into gangs or other criminal activity while behind bars, and end up with new charges and a longer prison stay than what they were originally sentenced with.

Some men, about two percent, stay behind "The Walls" for the rest of their lives. Charles Manson, the infamous cult leader who orchestrated the Tate-Labianca murders in 1969, has lived most of his natural life behind bars, since boyhood. He will, almost certainly, die there.

Truly, crime does not pay.

If there is one common theme running through this volume, that is it.

Micajah and Wiley Harpe both died violent deaths at the hands of a posse. Micajah's skull was nailed to a tree.

Belle Gunness is believed to have perished violently in a fire. If she did not, she surely spent the rest of her life hiding in fear from the retribution that could have swooped down upon her at any time.

Herman Webster Mudgett, alias "H.H. Holmes," went to the gallows believing himself to be, literally, turning into the devil.

John Dillinger was gunned down by law enforcement, after being led to his sorry fate by the Woman in Red.

Richard Loeb was stabbed to death while attempting the homosexual rape of a fellow inmate. Nathan Leopold was eventually released from prison at a very advanced age, after his entire youth and life and all his potential had been, essentially, wasted.

Ed Gein died confined to a state psychiatric hospital.

Charlie Starkweather went to the electric chair.

Richard Speck died in prison, a grotesquerie with hormonally augmented breasts who was, obviously, desperately mentally sick.

John Wayne Gacy was executed by lethal injection at Menard State Prison in Illinois in 1993.

Jeffrey Dahmer was beaten to death by fellow inmate Christopher Scarver while he was cleaning a toilet. He was serving a life sentence without parole.

Jim Jones (not profiled here) blew his brains out in a paranoid frenzy, after a veritable orgy of murder and mass suicide. Above his dead body was a sign hanging. That sign read: Those who do not remember the past are condemned to repeat it. The quote is attributed to George Santayana. In the case of nearly every criminal, truer words were never spoke.

Crime does not pay.

Currently 35 U.S. states have the death penalty. While we are almost certain that none of our readers will ever sink to the depths plumbed by the human demons we have profiled in our book, it would do every young man or woman good to remember that there have been 1,193 executions since the death penalty was reinstated (to date).

Even though we know (?) that there are no murderers reading this book, we also know many people will one day consider picking up a bottle, a needle, or even a gun. They may be considering robbery or worse. They may just not be cautious enough while under the influence.

To them we would like to leave the parting images:

The gas chamber.

The gallows.

The firing squad.

The lethal needle shoved into an arm.

The stabbing death.

The brains beat out by a fellow inmate.

The electric chair.

The cold concrete and steel hallways where so many millions of men live out their pointless, torturous lives, listening to the ticking of the clocks, and dreading tomorrow.

So look long and hard down that long, hard road before you travail there. Because, once you pick the pathway of crime, there is usually no coming back.

A word to the wise guy.

Bibliographic Note:

Some of the books that helped the most with the preparation of this volume were:

Bloodletters and Badmen by Jay Robert Nash
Deviant and Depraved by Harold Schechter
The Last Victim by Jason Moss, and
Cannibal Killers by Peter Haining.

Also, many fine websites proved to be instrumental in researching various aspects of these cases.

One of the most valuable was www.trutv.com.